MONEY-MAKING MEETINGS

MONEY-MAKING MEETINGS

*Ninety-Seven Keys
to Marketing Your Knowledge
in the Multi-Million Dollar
Workshop and Seminar Industry*

By

WILLIAM G. WILLIAMS

SHARE PUBLISHING COMPANY
P.O. Box 3453, Annapolis, MD 21403

ISBN: 0-933344-02-3

Share Success Series

Contents

Preface

I once knew a fire marshal who conducted an annual fire prevention seminar at a community college where I served as director of community services. The fire marshal planned the content of the seminars and arranged for all speakers, films, and handouts. He provided the names of likely participants, promoted the meetings, and was the principal instructor. Thirty-five to fifty persons paid $25.00 each to attend the seminars, and each offering of the meeting earned $400 to $600 after expenses. The fire marshal accepted $100 for his efforts. I placed the profits in the account of my community college which sponsored the seminars.

The fire marshal was an expert on fire safety, performed nearly all of the work, and accepted a majority of the responsibility for each meeting. We at the college did little other than to place a newspaper advertisement, print and mail a few posters, call the motel, and collect the money. The fire marshal accepted a small percentage of the profits because he had only one of two necessary meeting skills: (1) subject knowledge, and (2) conference management knowledge. Without both these elements of success in meeting sponsorship, he was forced to become an employee — rather than an entrepreneur.

He did not realize he could sponsor his own meeting. He also did not know that he could repeat his meeting in other cities, or that he could franchise his meeting for sale to other sponsors across the country. He did not see the market for tape recordings and handouts from his meeting which could be sold by mail order. Again, he was an expert in his field of knowledge, but he did not understand conference management.

The fire marshal is not alone. Thousands of experts sell their knowledge through schools and colleges at a small fraction of its true value to the public. Many thousands more do not sell their knowledge at all. This book is intended to help readers build the knowledge and confidence needed to sponsor profitable meetings, so that they can sell their knowledge directly to buyers.

Conference management is a multi-million dollar industry, and there are thousands of potential new meeting sponsors who could join this lucrative field, given an opportunity to learn more about successful meeting sponsorship. Profitable meetings can produce earnings which greatly exceed the salaries or professional fees of sponsors. Meetings can also enhance a business, a professional practice, or a salaried career. In addition, meeting sponsorship produces some attractive tax deduction opportunities for such things as home office use and automobile use. A special attraction for salaried persons is receiving earnings which have not been subject to deductions for retirement, life insurance or health plans.

This book contains 97 suggestions, each followed by brief explanations, related ideas, and examples. The suggestions are opinions based on my years of conference management experience. I have tried to include all important considerations in managing a meeting, but sponsors should expect to improvise in their own unique situations.

In this book I use several terms almost interchangeably for variety. "Meeting," "conference," "seminar," and "workshop," are all words used to describe the same thing except where I am discussing their differences. Persons who pay to attend meetings are referred to as "participants," "registrants," or "the audience."

The Author

William G. Williams is a veteran conference manager and advisor whose experience includes more than 200 meetings on a great variety of topics. He is an expert on a wide range of meeting formats and all phases of meeting planning, advertising, presentation, and evaluation.

Dr. Williams earned his Bachelor of Arts and Master of Arts at George Washington University, and his Doctor of Philosophy at Florida State University. He has held administrative positions in the Virginia Community College System, at George Washington University, and at Georgetown University.

He is the author of four books and twelve articles, and is a consultant on educational marketing and conference management.

SECTION ONE

THE GREAT POTENTIAL OF
MONEY-MAKING MEETINGS

SECTION ONE

1. Develop an understanding of the money-making meeting concept.

In this book we will be considering the management of meetings sponsored by individuals, organizations, business firms, and government agenices, for the purpose of earning profits from paid admissions. The admission fee is paid by members of the audience in exchange for valuable information or skills. A typical money-making meeting is conducted in a motel meeting room, and is promoted by direct mail and periodical advertising.

An example of this type of meeting is one held at various sites across the Nation on the subject of how to establish a consulting practice. The meeting sponsor is a successful consultant and at his meeting he presents suggestions based on his consulting experience. He also provides contract forms, report forms and other materials. He charges $105 per registrant and reports to have enrolled more than 9,000 persons — that is nearly one million dollars in gross income.

There are hundreds or even thousands of possible meeting topics including tax tricks, nutrition, investments, personal law, natural childbirth, sales techniques, advertising, home safety, and energy conservation. Each reader will have individual subject priorities.

Conventions and other meetings of peers are not the principal focus of my suggestions, but rather meetings at which experts sell techniques for success to others who have far less ability. This is where the greatest possibilities for high earnings exist.

There is nothing new about profit-making conferences; they constitute a large industry with many imaginative and aggressive conference sponsors. This book is designed to inform and encourage new sponsors or to enhance the skills of existing sponsors.

3

2. Consider the earnings potential of a money-making meeting.

One meeting sponsor charges $375 for a two-day seminar on marketing. With a mere 35 participants he will gross over $13,000 in two days. His production costs to run the meeting are perhaps $2,000. His advertising costs are low due to the appeal of his topic to a very specific audience. He can send flyers to several thousand prospective registrants and advertise in several carefully selected journals for less than $1,000.

I would not attend or sponsor such a high-priced meeting, but it can be done and is rather commonplace. If you are a solar energy expert, you might charge $45 for a one-day meeting. With 40 persons in the audience you could net a profit of $500 to $700 based on a gross admissions revenue of $1,800. For many middle income persons $500 to $700 represents a week's pay in one day.

So here we have a range of expectations — from $500 to $5,000 per day from money-making meetings.

We will cover budgeting in more detail in another section, but for now I must point out that the financial risk of meetings is not great because the production costs need not be incurred if the meeting is not successfully enrolled.

3. Understand the investment advantages of money-making meetings.

A meeting sponsor need not have a payroll, an office outside the home, an inventory, or any fixed financial obligations associated with the meeting. You need no special certificate or particular type of education. There are no warehouses or delivery trucks, no sales agents or showrooms.

What you will need is planning ability, teaching skill, leadership capacity, and ideas to sell — information, skills, abilities, or techniques that other persons desire enough to acquire them from you at a price. Also required is an investment for meeting promotion

4

(advertising) which you cannot recover if your meeting fails to attract an audience sufficiently large to hold the meeting.

4. Compare other ways to sell your knowledge.

Meeting sponsorship has several advantages over other methods of selling knowledge. Consulting, for example, can involve more travel and more persuasion headaches. The consultant's headaches come from involvement in organizational stress, personality conflicts, power struggles, and policy disputes. Members of a conference audience step out of their workplace behavior setting, while the consultant often steps into a workplace setting with its existing competition for dominance and resources. Few consultants earn between $500 and $5,000 per day, a possibility mentioned in Suggestion 2 as earnings for meeting sponsors.

Compared with writing a book as a means to sell your knowledge, the profitable conference is far less tedious and time consuming. Much of book authorship involves editing, re-writing, manuscript preparation, revisions, negotiations with publishers, and then waiting many months for small royalties. You can plan a meeting in as little as two weeks and conduct the meeting within a few months. It may require a year or more to write a book, a year to find a publisher after several contacts and book changes, and a year or more for the publisher to release the book. Writers often lose control over book content and promotion. Royalties are only 10 to 15 percent of the retail price. A book can be a good conference byproduct, but is not nearly so desirable as a meeting series or franchise.

You can sell your knowledge as a teacher at a college, university, or high school adult education center. This is good experience and a valuable professional asset, but the educational administrators and their governing boards will make certain that you do not get rich from teaching. Teachers can earn between $400 and $1,200 for a 15-week class. If you have the potential to sponsor a money-making meeting, you will prefer to earn more in a shorter time span, and be your own boss.

5

5. Consider the possibilities for follow-up earnings.

If your meeting makes good money in Toledo, it could be repeated in Cleveland, Akron, Youngstown, Columbus, Dayton, and Cincinnati. You could then go outside of Ohio to hundreds of similar markets in other states. Each time you repeat your meeting, preparation time and costs should decrease as you gain ability and efficiency. For example, your advertising could promote several meetings at once, cutting promotional costs per meeting.

If you tire of traveling and repeating the same program, you could hire several employees to offer the meetings or franchise your meeting as a business opportunity. Franchise holders would send you 10 to 20 percent of their total fees in exchange for your instructions, tape recordings, lesson plans, and handout samples. The franchise holder would pay an initial acquisition fee, and be bound by a contract which would protect your rights to the meetings.

Another follow-up earnings possibility is the sale of tape recordings and meeting handouts by mail order to persons who cannot attend your meeting. The sponsor of the $105 consultant practice seminar mentioned in Suggestion 1 sells tapes and handouts for about $85 by mail order. Selling 500 such packets each year as a sideline totals $52,500 gross income.

If you are sincerely interested in writing a book, you will find the task much easier after your meetings have been conducted. You can contact several publishers and tell them of your success with meetings and franchises. Try to find a publisher who will assign a ghost writer to work from your tapes and materials. An author's agent can help negotiate such favorable terms. You need not write or edit one word if you have something valuable to offer — based on meeting success.

Your successful conference can stimulate vigorous new interest in your business or professional practice. New customers or clients can be acquired based on your publicity or meeting contacts. You might be promoted on your job or find a better job — if you still want one.

SECTION TWO

MAKING THE MOST OF YOUR MEETING

6. Identify your type of meeting.

For the purposes of this book, a money-making meeting is one which is held for a few hours to several days and which can be devoted to one of a large variety of topics such as time management, supervision, starting a business, investing, or hundreds of other possibilities. Most such topics are designed to help participants with their job performance, career prospects, personal lives, hobby enjoyment, financial success, and family relationships.

Participants learn of the meetings through newspaper advertisements, direct mail, association newsletters, and word of mouth. The participants pay a fee to the meeting sponsor ranging from $25 to $150 per day. This fee includes meals and refreshments, occasionally includes lodgings, but rarely transportation. Ten to 100 or more persons may attend.

Most meeting sponsors and participants are not well aware of the various classifications of meetings to which such terms as "workshop," "seminar," "institute," "meeting," "conference," and "class" apply. These terms are used almost interchangeably for most practical purposes, but the distinctions should be known. A workshop includes an activity such as completing tax forms or bandaging first aid patients. A seminar is a small group session offering discussion and the exchange of information. An institute is what I have described in the two paragraphs above and most money-making meetings are institutes — though I do not advise use of the term because it is rarely used and is easily confused with "institution." A meeting or a conference involves an association or a business organization membership and an implied sharing of ideas to reach a consensus. A class is held for brief periods of time on a succession of dates as in the case of a college class.

You may observe that these brief definitions cause problems because they cannot be applied strictly in public use. The solution is to use "meeting," "conference," "seminar," or "workshop," and then add a further explanation such as "lecture with films and demonstrations," even though you may actually be offering an institute.

I hope you will not call your program a seminar if it is a lecture to 100 persons, or designate it as a workshop if there is to be no practical hands-on activity. Such technical errors in terminology are very common, however, and of no great consequence unless some participant complains about false expectations.

I wish there were well-defined and widely understood terms, but there are not.

7. Assess the value of your topic.

In a money-making meeting you will be selling knowledge, skills, motivation, or attitude change. What are they worth? Would a person take a day off from work or give up a day off, drive 30 miles or buy an airline ticket, possibly rent a room, and pay $50 to hear you explain how to appeal a real estate zoning decision or classify job descriptions? How about $150 for two days? Would the participant's employer pay for it?

You cannot often depend on intellectual curiosity as a motivation, and you will rarely have academic credit to offer. The potential registrants must value your program much more than its expense and inconvenience, and you must create and render such value. In order to earn money, your topic must be worth money.

Another way to build enrollment enthusiasm is to offer a controversial topic, or even arrange a confrontation of special interests concerning, for example, nuclear radiation dangers, toxic wastes, or taxation. I prefer to sell valuable information and skills rather than encounter or debate, but readers will have a wide variety of abilities, interests, and potential topic ideas.

In any event, plan to have each member of your audience gain $500 worth of benefit for every $100 in fees and other expenses.

Remember that you will want to repeat a profitable meeting, so offer value the first time.

Potential registrants for your meeting will spend their employer's money and time more readily than they will sacrifice their own. Others things being equal, an employer-valued topic is five times more attractive than a citizen-valued topic. If the boss says go, they go — expenses paid. But, a warning here: the "sent" participant can be less attentive and more difficult to lead.

8. Assess your knowledge or talent to be offered for sale.

Make a list of topics on which you are an expert. The topics could be related to your career, hobbies, or personal life. Your topic might be domestic relations law, stocks and bonds, or antiques, depending on your training and experience. Concentrate on the two or three topics you know best. Remember, while you may hire a meeting associate, a consultant, or other helpers to assist you at your meeting, you must have the capacity for total self-reliance. You must be nearly omnipotent within the scope of the meeting content. If you are puzzled by questions and comments at your meeting, it could turn out to be a very long day.

9. Assess your teaching skills.

Do you have formal classroom teaching experience? Do you have public speaking experience related to civic groups, church activities, or professional associations? Do you often train employees or explain procedures to the public? Are you confident in front of a group? (Nervous is okay.) Can you explain a complex topic to thirty or more persons and answer their questions for four, six, or more hours?

You need not apply for a conference management license. There is no personnel director to screen the self-employed. Therefore, wise self-selection is important.

10. Do not explore too far for a conference topic.

Unless you wish to become a conference broker (sponsor other persons' meetings) your money-making conference idea is inside your mind right now. While there might be a large potential audience for a workshop on how to buy a good used car, lose weight, or start a business, if you are not a thorough expert on such topics you cannot offer them.

You will need to study the range of your knowledge in order to discover its attractive aspects. A body of knowledge needs refinement and targeting to public needs. Anything which enhances a person's career, economic status, or happiness can be a good conference subject. For example, a head nurse at a hospital might offer a meeting on the rights of hospital patients, or how to plan for and make the best use of hospital care. A pest exterminator could sponsor a workshop on pest identification and control by homeowners, the regulation and selection of pesticides, or how to identify extermination problems requiring attention from the trade.

What part of what you know could be of value to a potential audience? Ten thousand readers of this book may have as many or more topics or special treatments of topics. Turn your idea around and look at it from varied perspectives, but always from the angle of what information the public will buy, and what you realistically can provide. You might be an expert in home renovations and additions, but the public might not buy carpentry skills because a person who will attempt such projects probably already has the required skills. What you could sell in this case perhaps is the knowledge of how to obtain permits, comply with building codes, and acquire approval of the electrical and plumbing installations.

11. Assess your leadership skills.

Are you a leader? Do colleagues seek you out for advice and support? Do your friends and neighbors seem interested in your work or hobbies? Do they ask you questions or seek your help? Do others turn to you to solve problems? Can you persuade? Do others follow your advice? Are you now a consultant, counselor, or other person paid to furnish ideas and evaluations?

Your leadership status will be boosted at your meeting simply by means of the position you hold at the speaker's table. Your venturesome spirit in being the initiator of the meeting, rather than a respondent, will place you above and apart from the audience. A real leader will make such dominance very subtle.

Guard against basing your leadership confidence on past experiences in which you have had an institutional dominance not supported by your own personal charisma. For example, Captain Jack, the uniformed police officer who talks to elementary school pupils on traffic safety may develop a false sense of leadership. So too, a medical school admissions director will not likely face many leadership challenges among the 3,000 applicants who write or visit to court one of the 100 openings in the first-year class.

Finally, a group of strangers will usually be easier to lead than persons already acquainted with you and with each other.

12. Assess your credentials and your reputation.

When the public learns of a meeting they will try to evaluate its leader. Do you have a strong reputation in your field of knowledge, or a reputation which can be created through promotional literature. Do you have college degrees, professional society membership, elective offices, special honors, publications, successful projects, a long list of references, business success, or some other distinction you can boast of?

In the conference business you will be selling yourself. List the truthful statements about yourself which you can use to build confidence and high expectations in the minds of prospective registrants. One man I know who has taught dozens of workshops on home energy conservation has specific data on how he dramatically reduced his home energy costs. He can publish "before and after" utility bills. The records are his credentials, and former participants at his workshop are his reputation.

13. Consider assisting another meeting sponsor.

Potential meeting sponsors who lack experience in teaching and group leadership may wish to assist with the meetings of other sponsors before offering their own. Local motels and temporary employment agencies may know of conference leaders seeking assistance, especially those from out of town. The continuing education office or conference bureau at a nearby college or university may need help or give you the names of sponsors you can contact directly. Any time you see a conference advertised you could telephone or write the sponsor to offer your services.

The amount of payment you receive for helping with the meeting is insignificant compared with the knowledge you will gain. You may be required to volunteer, although I do not recommend that you accept volunteers at your own meeting. Take notes at the meeting on which parts of the program were successful and which were unsuccessful — from facilities to audience reactions. Study these notes so that you can use your observations to improve your own meeting plans.

14. Investigate organizations and agencies related to your topic.

It is important that you become aware of citizen groups and government agencies related to your meeting topic. For example, if your topic is in the real estate field, a related organization would be the Board of Realtors and a related agency would be the real estate commission. By contacting organizations and agencies you might be able to recruit their members and employees for enrollment at your meeting. Also, they could be helpful with publicity and could recommend speakers.

I will discuss later the danger of giving away your meeting idea and how to avoid revealing your exact plans when you discuss your meeting.

14

15. Study the conference competition.

Readers of this book who are true experts in their fields of knowledge will often be aware of existing workshops in their subject areas. For example, a professional consultant likely will have attended or heard of existing conferences on how to establish a consulting practice. If you have never heard of a conference sponsor operating in your area of expertise there may be none. If you have no knowledge of existing conferences, others will also be unaware and will be prospective registrants for your meeting. Check old copies of your professional journals or hobby magazines. Ask friends if they know of available workshops — without revealing your exact plans.

Conference sponsors must become aware of the instructional offerings of colleges, universities, high school adult education departments, recreation departments and other sources of classroom instruction. Write or telephone for course listings, without revealing your exact plans — you do not want to give away a good idea. Keep in mind that it is difficult to compete with tax-supported and tax-exempt institutions. Their tuition rates and public recognition are very attractive. Also, they are often accredited and can offer transferable academic credit.

Books and magazines can compete with money-making meetings. Referring again to the consulting conference, there are now at least two books available on the subject. I would certainly try a $15 book before attending an expensive conference on the same subject. At your public library look up your meeting subject and title in *Books in Print* to determine if there are competing books. Also look up a variety of related topics. *Writer's Market* and *Literary Market Place* have useful lists and descriptions of magazines.

16. Consider some of the negative ramifications of your meeting.

Once you have decided on a specific topic, ask yourself who

would be reluctant to have the public better informed on the topic. Who might consider the offering of such information to be their exclusive domain? If you sponsor a meeting on how to appeal real estate assessments or how to demand public school instruction in a language other than English, you can expect to make some enemies or at least arouse suspicion. Would such conflicts be serious enough to cause you to cancel your meeting, move it to another location, or seek prior approval?

Perhaps you could visit the person whose reaction might be unfriendly. The real estate assessor or school official in the above examples might be visited in order to obtain their reactions to your plans. Do not reveal the exact nature of your plans or you could find that the assessor or educator will announce their sponsorship of your meeting idea the following week. If you seem uncertain of your intentions you may obtain a tentative approval which will be difficult for them to retract once you have made firm plans for your meeting. By contrast, the presentation of a formal proposal could be intimidating and earn one of those "you should have met with us first — I will have to take this to our board" reactions.

17. Do not talk about your exact plans.

As you contemplate sponsoring a financially successful meeting you must not discuss your exact topic or your specific plans with anyone! Of course, sooner or later you must announce your offering formally, but do not give any undue advance notice. Conference sponsorship is a multi-million dollar business, with hundreds of operators. Many conference sponsors are looking for more good ideas wherever they can be found. There may also be persons, organizations, and agencies in your community willing to compete with you merely for the recognition or the opportunity to express their own viewpoints. Competitors without financial motivation are especially dangerous because they can rob you of your audience with low pricing regardless of any other advantage you might offer.

If you wish to discuss your meeting with an attorney, account-ant, motel manager, or officials of some organization or agency re-lated to your topic, do not reveal your exact plans or topic beyond the minimum which must be discussed. You could mention that you do not really believe your idea will be popular or that it is a ter-rible risk. I find that when I have a very promising idea I cannot keep from bragging about it, so I shade the truth a bit and brag about some other similar idea.

18. Limit your publicity.

I have indicated several times earlier that you must not reveal your specific plans because of the dangers of motivating competi-tion. I wish to stress this again. In order to maximize the success of your meeting you must be warned to use only as much publicity as you need to successfully sell attendance at your meeting. You must not reveal your plans until your offering is ready, or nearly ready.

An advertisement in the *Wall Street Journal* or the *New York Times* will announce your conference topic to the world, including compe-titors. I might steal your idea! Remember, you cannot copyright an idea, only the form of its expression. If you were selling a new toy, you could make thousands and dominate the market, but you can-not mass-produce meetings. So limit your publicity to your ability to respond to the market. Why create a market for someone else?

I will have more advice to offer on this and other aspects of pro-motion in Section Six.

19. Be prepared to take full advantage of your meeting idea.

If you wish to be a successful meeting sponsor, you must have contingency plans for devoting your full-time efforts to the rapid expansion of your conference offering. If your conference is a big success, you cannot plan to offer one meeting each year for ten years. I know of persons who tried to go slow in order to obtain a steady income from an instructional topic over several years — often for income tax purposes. Some of these persons were unwilling to give up the security of a steady, full-time job or business. Others sought an easy pace of life. I talked with one such person the very day I was editing this section of the book, and he told me he wanted to get back into the action again. I could not tell him, but there are several other hungrier persons who have now dominated "the action."

You must be ready to take advantage of the full market potential of your money-making idea. If your meeting earns big money in Davenport or Denver, go national. Be ready to expand through your own travel, the appointment of staff presenters, franchising your meeting, or the sale of tape recordings and handouts.

20. Become a meeting expert.

As I have noted, a successful meeting sponsor needs two kinds of knowledge: (1) knowledge of the conference topic and, (2) knowledge of the conference business. The second part will be the greater challenge for most meeting sponsors, because most conference management knowledge will be relatively new, while the meeting topic knowledge may have been acquired throughout a lifetime.

In Sections One and Two of this book I have tried to describe the great potential of money-making meetings and methods for maximizing the success of a meeting sponsor. I have also posted some danger signs with the hope that readers will benefit from them.

The following sections become increasingly detailed and operational, from testing meeting equipment to coping with troublesome personalities in your audience — from spare projector bulbs to luncheon menus and meeting rehearsals. I will try to cover lessons learned from all the successes and failures I have experienced or witnessed at hundreds of meetings, and give you much of the insight I wish I had possessed when I first started out with meetings many years ago.

SCHEDULING AND LOCATING MEETINGS
FOR BEST RESULTS

SECTION THREE

21. Start in your own city or state, if appropriate.

Beginning conference sponsors will find many advantages in holding their first few meetings in their own communities. A meeting in a sponsor's community will be easier to conduct, there will be lower transportation costs, and there will be fewer problems with meeting room arrangements. A local meeting room can be visited, friends and colleagues can assist, and the conference sponsor will better be able to avoid scheduling conflicts, such as local pageants, for example. You, the sponsor, will also be more certain of the applicability of the meeting's content. For example, the content of a real estate seminar such as zoning, taxes, and vacancy rates varies from city to city.

A local meeting also provides easier contact with members of the audience if there is a need to reschedule or divide the meeting. You will have easier access to knowledge of meeting site area rules regarding a business license or any special taxes. If you operate a business or professional office, your staff and equipment will be nearby, and the meeting can stimulate interest in your business or professional practice.

22. Consider the disadvantages of a local site.

When you are operating in your home community you cannot be nearly so flamboyant or controversial as when you are in a distant town for a one-day show. There is also the common belief that a true expert must come from at least 500 miles away. If you make a mistake or offer criticism, the persons involved will be your neighbors, not strangers you will never see again.

Your topic may not be of local interest or you may not have the population or travel conveniences to attract a sufficient audience near home. Your area of residence may not have the prestige or accommodations needed to attract persons to a national or regional meeting — compare Boonesboro with Boston, for example. Your climate or entertainment attractions may not be suitable.

23. Select distant sites based on population centers, transportation centers, and interest centers.

We are dealing here with three different concepts. First, attracting commuters from a local population. Second, attracting travelers from several states, a region, or the entire Nation by means of good transportation. Third, selecting a site which is attractive to persons with career or hobby interests related to your topic.

A meeting based on population will attract commuters who live within driving distance of the meeting site. For this audience, good road access and parking are required. The site should be on a major highway — not "take a left at Loving Lane, then a sharp right at Glendale Road to the wooden bridge, then. . . ." The site could be between two population centers such as Baltimore and Washington, D.C. if a large population base is needed. A typical topic for a population site meeting is of a general interest nature such as dieting or parenting.

A meeting at a transporation center will serve a larger geographical area and might be held at an airport motel. An entire multi-state area is served in this way and the population north, south, east, and west along air passenger routes should be calculated. Saint Louis, Memphis, Atlanta, and Dallas are good examples of regional transporation centers, while Chicago is probably the best national center. A topic offered at a regional or national transportation center could be one for which price or specialized interest will limit the response rate to such a level that you will need access to a very large population. General interest meetings, such as our dieting and parenting examples will suffer in a transportation center due to travel costs and over-exposure to population.

The third type of center is chosen to appeal to the hobby or professional interests of prospective enrollees. A meeting for publishers would be held in New York City, while a meeting for federal government workers would be held in the Washington, D.C. area. A yachting topic would be offered in Annapolis or San Francisco.

24. Avoid conference sites near state or other governmental boundaries, in some cases.

If you are offering a meeting topic which is influenced by local laws or government services, the inclusion of participants from different political subdivisions can create problems. Either your information will not apply uniformly to all members of the audience, or you will need to present numerous qualifications and explanations suiting the various governments. A conference in Chattanooga would be geographically attractive to persons in five states — Tennessee, North Carolina, South Carolina, Georgia, and Alabama, together with scores of counties and cities. It would be difficult to discuss local tax laws at such a site.

Multiple explanations will stagnate the flow of your meeting, bore your audience, and confuse speakers.

25. Choose a good response rate month.

The time of year chosen to schedule a meeting is very important. People respond to instructional offerings in different ways according to the season. I have found conference response rates to be high in April and October. Late March is also good, as well as late September and early November. Late January and all of February are attractive for southern resort locations if your publicity does not arrive with the Christmas and Hanukkah mail.

Thanksgiving through New Year's is out due to holidays. Evaluate the possibility of ice and snow at northern sites in the winter months. A blizzard may give you plenty of time at home to send refund checks, but it will be painful. Late May, through the summer, to mid-September is a time for getting in and out of school, gardening, fishing, and travel for many potential members of your audience.

Minds turn to serious thoughts in the fall, and to renewal in the spring. Winter and summer are far less responsive except at resort sites. There are seasonal trends for specific meeting subjects. You cannot teach gun safety during parts of October or November; your audience is out in the woods and fields. Farming topics do well in the winter, but not during the growing season.

26. Find out how to conduct business in distant areas.

Before you conduct a meeting in a distant county, city, or state, seek advice from attorneys, government officials, or convention bureaus at the site in order to comply with local regulations on taxation and licensing. Motel managers and chambers of commerce can also be helpful, and if your successful meeting goes on the road you will begin to recognize and anticipate recurring business formalities.

I will describe later the use of a local coordinator for each distant meeting site. The coordinator can obtain information on local laws and regulations, as well as assist you with meeting room selection and publicity.

27. Avoid scheduling conflicts.

Buy a good calendar showing all the holidays including the more obscure ones such as Columbus Day and Lee-Jackson Day. In some locations a conference scheduled for the first week of the various hunting seasons will not be popular. Avoid state and federal tax return filing deadlines and the days prior to them. Athletic tournaments and local festivals can also present serious attendance problems.

Information on possible conflicts can be obtained from hotel and motel managers, chambers of commerce, newspapers, radio and television news rooms, and school athletic departments. Professional associations, trade groups, hobby clubs, and special interest organizations can identify dates which will serve their members well.

28. Consider a time and site which serves participants at another meeting.

A meeting held the day before or the day after a related conference in the same location can attract many participants who can combine the two events in one travel budget. Educational consultants commonly hold conferences just before or just after conventions of educators in the same or nearby hotels. Your money-making meeting need not be endorsed by the sponsors of the other meeting, but it is valuable to try for cooperation. Most persons will assume there is some connection between the two meetings, unless your failure to cooperate causes retaliation by leaders of the other group.

I would not go so far as to have my meeting become part of the other conference program, because I might lose full control and be required to share revenue. The hotel reservation card you furnish with your promotional mailings or registration confirmation might well cover the entire period of both meetings. This policy will be helpful to the hotel or motel staff and to the members of your audience, as well as supporting the notion that the two meetings are a desirable package.

29. Choose a productive daily and hourly schedule.

Beginners should avoid offering a meeting of more than one day if at all possible. A meeting lasting two days or more with overnight accommodations introduces many additional responsibilities. As sponsor you become almost a captain of a ship or parent of a family at a multi-day meeting. You will be more involved with hospitality, meals, entertainment, questions, and personality conflicts.

A one-day meeting provides a tremendous amount of time for information and interaction and requires far less skill than a longer meeting. It is more impersonal — the participants arrive in the morning, they get out in the evening, and you go home at night. Lunch is the only meal to arrange, and luncheons are quite simple compared with dinners. Dinners involve a change of clothes, a cocktail hour, a quality menu, and an evening event.

Nine a.m. to 5 p.m. is a common one-day schedule, with variations such as 9:30 to 4:30. I suggest that you also consider 1 p.m. to 6 p.m., especially for commuter meetings. One o'clock to six o'clock provides only two hours less time than a full day meeting. There is no luncheon, and participants can drive to the meeting in the morning, or spend part of the morning at home or office if they are very near.

30. Plan for optional meeting days.

It is often wise to schedule two or three meeting dates in case there are more respondents than can be accommodated at one meeting. For example, you might schedule two or three consecutive Wednesdays so that some of the registrants can be contacted and rescheduled for the alternative dates. Over-enrollment is, of course, a fortunate situation, and it would be disappointing to have to return admission fees because you have no expansion plans. In the case of a distant meeting the optional days should be immediately after the published date in order to avoid travel cost and inconvenience for you and your staff.

The optional dates should not be published because such notification will split the registrants into two or three small groups. I prefer to be honest with the motel or other meeting room management and tell them that some of the reservations are merely optional overflow dates. The manager may refuse to reserve on that basis or specify a notification date by which you must cancel or confirm your extra reservations. The meeting staff, film rentals, and other arrangements should also be made for the optional dates.

SECTION FOUR

HELP FROM THE MEETING TEAM

SECTION FOUR

31. Appoint a meeting associate.

A "meeting associate" is a trusted and talented alter ego. A person to laugh at your jokes, defend your opinions, give attention to the audience, and perhaps lead parts of the meeting. This person will be for you what Ed McMahon is for Johnny Carson. A lone conference manager, especially when inexperienced, can be quite vulnerable. The mere presence of an associate can prevent problems before they occur.

The meeting associate might be a business partner, a close friend, a co-worker, or a club member. A chemisty professor sponsoring a meeting on everyday chemical hazards might select another chemistry instructor as an associate. In the case of a distant meeting the chemistry professor associate would be selected from the staff at a college in that area, but certainly not a complete stranger.

A meeting associate should be paid about $200 to $300 per day, or in IOUs for a similar favor such as editing a book or series of articles. I would not use a volunteer associate due to the demands and commitment involved.

The associate must be thoroughly trained and rehearsed. He or she must be fully knowledgeable in the subject area, but preferably not a person who is likely to become a competitor. This person should have good personal relations skills and provide a balance for some of your traits. If you are rather aggressive, the associate should be somewhat passive. If you are not at all humorous, the associate might be something of a clown.

A meeting associate is also a witness who is always present and can verify your version of what takes place at the meeting. For example, the associate could refute a claim that at a tax seminar you told participants to threaten or bribe IRS agents.

32. Employ one clerical assistant for each thirty participants.

Clerical assistants write receipts, give directions, hand out folders, find ash trays, and operate projectors. They also protect your doughnuts from passersby, and answer routine questions. They are the busy bees who make it possible for you to focus on meeting content and delivery, as well as audience reactions. It is quite important that assistants have good hospitality skills and attitudes. If I were forced to choose between personality and competence, I would prefer personality. Clerical assistants might be selected from your office staff, a temporary employment agency, or a college placement office.

The assistants should be familiar with the meeting schedule and content, and should take part in the meeting rehearsal. They should be able to answer questions and not come running for you each time a question is asked.

33. Appoint a local coordinator for distant meetings.

It is often necessary or desirable to hold a meeting at a location far from your own community, but it can then be difficult to make meeting room arrangements, anticipate scheduling conflicts, and provide local publicity. A "local coordinator" will be very helpful in this situation and can also serve as your meeting associate.

Let us assume that you live in Galveston where you have offered several successful lectures on sailboat racing rules and strategy. You wish to expand to Tampa. A yacht broker or racer in Tampa could be called upon to find a meeting room, help with local publicity, and hire clerical assistants. The local coordinator will know of scheduling conflicts such as a boat show, may have good promotional contacts, can visit facilities, enroll friends, and inquire about business legalities. Your attempts to coordinate a far distant site would be very difficult without the coordinator, who will also save you expensive trips to the site. A boat dealer, marine insurance agent, marina manager, or sailmaker might be willing to coordinate merely for the endorsement of having their names on your program and in your advertising.

If you are an expert in your field, you will know or can identify other experts across the land. Again, you must be obscure about your exact plans as long as possible, and try to find a coordinator who will not run away with your idea.

34. Involve other helpers in your meeting.

"Other helpers" are persons who can add to the content of your program, but who are actually serving their own goals. The helpers might be sales agents for products related to your topic, such as smoke alarms or fire extinguishers in the case of a fire safety meeting. At the same meeting another helper might be a government fire prevention official lecturing on new laws or new technology. You do not normally pay fees or expenses to other helpers because your meeting serves their interests. They do not pay the admission fee, but they do receive meals and handouts. They are not volunteers; it is their business to be at meetings.

In order to insure valuable contributions from helpers you must check on the quality of their past performance or have them explain their presentation plans in detail. Ask around to learn of their general reputation. I once used a state health official without knowing that he had previously alienated members of the medical community. His participation was not helpful, but I learned a lesson.

35. Avoid partners or association presentations.

The true leader and entrepreneur who is capable of planning and conducting a profitable meeting needs help, but will not share

33

authority or profits. If your goal is to make money for another person or for an organization, then pursue that goal, but first be certain that such generosity is in your best interest and that of your family.

It may be that you cannot conduct a meeting without including your law firm or architectural firm partner. Perhaps you owe much to your club or association and feel it deserves to be the sponsor. I would avoid partners and organizations unless there are very compelling reasons to include them. Would they include you?

36. Consider the advantages and disadvantages of "experts."

Expert consultants are often hired to add specialized knowledge and prestige to a meeting. In your own meeting there may be one or two subject specialties with which you are not familiar, or you may be tempted to list a big-name consultant because you are not well known. For example, at a solar energy workshop you may wish to have an engineering professor on hand to answer questions on mathematical calculations for heat transfer and storage capacity. The name of the professor and university may lend distinction to your program.

In some situations expert consultants may be valuable, but many are high-priced, tend to intimidate or overshadow meeting sponsors, and can actually obscure the sponsor's talents.

Often you can structure your content to avoid an expert and so notify your audience. For example, in your advertising state "... does not cover the calculation of heat transfer in various materials resulting from temperature gradients."

37. Hold a rehearsal for the meeting team.

A rehearsal will provide or confirm the preparation of your faculty and staff. All members of the meeting team must know their roles and become familiar with all segments of the meeting. The clerical assistants must know how to register participants, operate projectors, and arrange teaching aids. Your associate and other helpers must know your content and you must know theirs.

The rehearsal will establish your expectations of performance, and you should quickly accept the resignation of any member of your team who resists the rehearsal or fails to take it seriously. All rehearsal members should take notes, perhaps in the margins of the meeting schedule. Memory is not good enough. Ask faculty and staff if they can anticipate problems in the meeting procedures.

Over the years I have come to expect some members of the faculty and staff of a meeting (especially consultants) to arrive stone cold, with absolutely no preparation. You cannot wait until 9 a.m. on the morning of the meeting to check preparations or to show each clerical assistant how to perform each task.

BUDGETING FOR SUBSTANTIAL PROFITS

SECTION FIVE

38. Estimate your front money.

By "front money" I mean any expenses paid or obligated prior to the time when registration fees can be earned. One great advantage of a money-making meeting as a business venture is that front money investment is low — limited chiefly to promotion and a few minor items such as the cost of this book, advance film rentals, and clerical supplies. Promotion is the big item in front costs, and can be divided into two categories — publicity and advertising.

Publicity builds public awareness of your meeting through techniques which are nearly cost free. These include press releases, radio public service announcements, telling friends, announcing your conference at a club meeting, or listing it in an association newsletter. We will not consider these unbudgeted techniques in this section.

Advertising is paid promotion. Advertising is done through direct mail, periodicals (newspapers, magazines and journals), posters, and radio-television.

I have found direct mail advertising to be the most productive technique. It can be targeted to receptive persons, can include much information, can include registration forms, and has other advantages I will cover in Section Six. Direct mail advertising costs between $200 and $300 per thousand depending on what is mailed, the class of postage, sources of mailing labels, and the number of pieces mailed. For budgeting purposes let us say that you will send 2,000 mailers at a cost of $498. ($60 per thousand for a printed mailer, $109.00 per thousand for bulk mail postage, $80 for bulk mail postal privileges, and $40 per thousand for labels from a mailing list firm — $120 + 218 + 80 + 80 = $498.) If your response rate from the mailer is only 2 percent, there will be 40 respondents. I will have much more to suggest on mailings; here we want a budget figure.

Advertisements in periodicals are either display ads or classi-fieds. Rates vary widely for newspapers, magazines, journals and newsletters according to the circulation and policies of individual periodicals. Let us plan on one journal display ad at $75 and three newspaper classified ads at $12 each under "Instruction," or "Boats for Sale" or "Marine Services" in the case of our yacht racing lecture example. In some papers you will only get one ad for $36. Periodi-cal advertising normally does not "pull" well, but let us assume five registrants.

Posters are often successful. You simply obtain 40 or 50 extra mailers and tack or tape them at boat supply stores, yacht clubs, yacht broker offices, marine insurance firms, and marinas. Of course, we are using our yachting lecture example again. We will assume that seven persons responded to your posters.

I know of only a few profitable conferences advertised by radio or television, so I will only mention them briefly. Call your local sta-tions and ask for a rate card if you are interested in the electronic media. I believe radio could work, depending on rates, and enough earning potential to cover the cost.

To sum up, we will spend $609 ($498 + 75 + 36 = $609) and register 52 participants. For the purpose of this hypothetical case, we will charge $35 for the conference with a resulting gross revenue of $1,820.

Remember, your free publicity may have sold out the con-ference, or perhaps you only needed to use 700 of your mailers. Or, you might need 4,000 mailers plus radio. Only experience can determine such outcomes for individual meetings.

39. Estimate your production costs.

Compared with the front money estimates for promotion, pro-duction cost estimates are rather predictable.

For a meeting of 50 persons, two clerical assistants will be re-quired at $50 each from a "temporaries" firm which takes care of payroll deductions and other details. A meeting associate should receive an honorarium of $200 for a one-day meeting. The hotel will serve a buffet luncheon for 60 persons (52 + staff) at $5.00 each, and refreshments will be $2.00 each (coffee and doughnuts plus afternoon colas and cookies). A meeting folder and production of ten pages of handouts will be $1.00 each, and we will rent a $30 movie or slide set. Your travel and lodging expenses would be added for a meeting in a distant city. Expenses vary from city to city, and inflation must also be considered. However, your admission fee can also be adjusted for location and inflation.

So, we pay $100 for clerical assistants, $200 to the meeting associate, $300 for lunch (60 × $5.00), $120 for refreshments (60 × $2.00), $60 for folders and contents, and $30 for a movie. That totals $810.

We estimated promotion costs at $609 and production costs are estimated at $810, so total costs are $1,419. Revenue is $1,820, resulting in a profit of $401. Most of us do not earn $400 for one or two days work, but we can do better. Some adjustments are needed.

Sample Conference Budgets

	Original	Change 1		Change 2
Front Money				
2000 Mailers	$ 498	1000 Mailers	$ 289	$ 289
Periodical Ads	111	No Ads		
Sub-Total	609		289	289
Production Money				
Two Assistants	100		100	100
Associate	200		200	200
Lunch	300	Lower Price	270	No Lunch
Refreshments	120	Lower Price	60	60
Folders & Handouts	60		60	60
Movie	30		30	30
Sub-Total	810		720	450
Total Costs	1,419		1,009	739
Gross Earnings	1,820		1,820	1,820
Profit	401		811	1,081
Profit with 35 participants	58 loss		327	520

40. Make adjustments for maximum profits.

If we rely heavily on low-cost publicity such as posters, personal contacts, and newsletter listings, we might be able to enroll 50 persons using only 1,000 mailers and no periodical advertising. This savings of $320 increases profits to $721. ($320 savings — $40 labels, $60 mailers, $109 postage, $111 ads).

To further increase profits we find a motel which will give us a package price of $4.50 per person on the buffet lunch, saving us $30 and we decide to supply our own coffee and colas at a cost of $1.00 per person rather than $2.00 which saves us another $60. Our two clerical assistants can easily take care of refreshments. We add $90 to the profit and we are over $800 to $811.

Are there other ways to increase revenue or decrease costs in this example? The size of the audience is large and the price is as high as it should go because we are offering a hobby subject. At a business meeting such as supervision or marketing $35 would be a low admission fee and it could be increased.

There is one other possibility for increasing net earnings — changing to a 1 p.m. to 6 p.m. format. Eliminating the luncheon ($270) will increase profits to $1,081.

Please notice that we did not tamper with the handouts, films, and the meeting team. Some things are necessary. A manufacturer cannot take the wheels off an automobile in order to increase profits.

What would happen if only 35 persons enrolled rather than 52? Earnings would decline by $595 and costs would drop due to 17 fewer meals, handouts, and refreshments. There would still be a $500 profit with the 1:00 p.m. to 6:00 p.m. schedule. This, and other results are shown in the sample conference budgets.

If our example meeting was on a business topic we could raise the price. A higher price could reduce the size of the audience, but earnings may not suffer, while costs could be reduced. Let us say that the price for a real estate meeting will be $55 and that attendance will drop to 35. Your gross income here of $1,925 ($55 × 35 = $1,925) is an increase over the $1,820 with the lower fee. Also, you will have 17 fewer meals, refreshments, and folders to pay for.

Thus, your profit would increase between $100 and $200, depending on whether you use an all-day schedule or the 1:00 p.m. to 6:00 p.m. format.

41. Set your fee so as not to belittle yourself or your audience.

A low price of $10 to $20 for a day-long meeting with lunch and refreshments suggests that you do not have much to offer or perhaps that you are trying to sell something extra at the meeting. Many persons will be suspicious and you could expect many telephone calls and much correspondence rather than registrations — lots of rejections too! Remember that a participant's cost of attending includes transportation, perhaps lodgings, and a day lost from work or family. Many will not make that kind of investment for $15 worth of meeting program.

Your price must not be so high as to make prospective customers feel ashamed to attend or embarrassed to ask their employers to pay the bill. I once learned of a very attractive two-day meeting in my field of interest, but the $350 price tag turned me away. Thirty-seven persons did attend I later learned, and they loved it. I suppose that when participants pay $350 they must love it, or feel like fools. There is an important lesson here on keeping your price a bit high.

A price on the high side also inclines participants to be serious and cooperative in order to achieve full benefits from the meeting. Low fees tend to result in tardiness and lack of concentration.

SECTION SIX

PRODUCTIVE ADVERTISING AND PUBLICITY

SECTION SIX

42. Start with limited promotion and escalate as needed.

Promotion is the most expensive and the most elastic cost in conference sponsorship. It is wise, especially for the first offering, to start with limited promotion, having additional advertising plans ready to carry out quickly as required. Please recall that promotion consists of publicity, which is nearly cost free, and advertising, which is paid promotion.

The first step is to tell friends, colleagues, clients, and customers in order to determine how many will attend. Then try other measures such as posters and newsletter notices. If advertising is needed to increase responses, mail 500 to 700 flyers and perhaps place an inexpensive newspaper advertisement. Later, you can increase your total mailings to 2,000 or 3,000 and place several more advertisements in order to fill your audience to the desired size.

To start out with a full mailing and periodical advertising program could waste money if it is not needed, and over-enrollment can be as big a problem as under-enrollment.

One conference sponsor I know started out with a small "teaser" advertisement in a newspaper which stated that he was considering forming a class and invited interested persons to telephone or write. A response of five or six persons to such a notice is a good sign to proceed with plans. This is a good way to test distant site responsiveness through the use of out-of-town newspapers. Of course, you must be prepared to move quickly so that others do not use your meeting idea.

One very favorable characteristic of direct mail advertising is that response rates, once established, are rather constant. If the first 500 mailers generate 10 responses, you can usually depend on a continued 2 per cent response rate, so that 2,000 mailers will generate 40 responses. If you establish a 4 percent response rate you will need only 1,000 mailers for 40 responses. However, a change in the mailer and the type of address list will alter the predictability, as will changes in such factors as location and dates of the meeting.

43. Schedule your promotion to last approximately four weeks, ending four weeks prior to the meeting.

A four-week promotional campaign ending four weeks prior to the meeting results in a lead time of about two months to one month for prospective registrants when they receive notification. This lead time will allow them to place the meeting on their calendars, but it is not so far in advance of the meeting date as to make the meeting seem intangible or remote. Also, the meeting is not so far in the future as to encourage them to put the notice aside, and perhaps lose it.

I prefer a three- to five-week promotional campaign simply because I do not wish to be occupied with this activity for longer periods. I also do not want to accept inquiries and registrations over a long period of time. Beginners will need five weeks, experienced meeting sponsors can use three.

Big conference promoters often list six to eight months of their meeting offerings in one notice. This violates our advice above, but the large operators have a full-time staff to handle responses and they achieve great advertising efficiency by reducing the cost of advertising per meeting.

44. Study direct mail advertising.

Any conference promotion plan should include a variety of promotional efforts such as posters, phone calls and classified advertising. Such promotion requires only common sense or the assistance of other persons such as a newspaper classified advertisement writer. It is fairly simple to have 50 posters printed and to tack or tape them at public places such as libraries and shopping centers. No special skill is required to inform friends, colleagues, or clients.

Direct mail advertising, usually the most productive form of promotion, does require special knowledge. There are four elements in a direct mail campaign: (1) the item to be mailed; (2) the addressees to whom it will be sent; (3) the postage; and (4) the processing of the mailers.

The item to be mailed must be written, designed, set in type, and printed. You prepare the "copy" or the printed message. It can then be given to a professional designer who will do the art work, typesetting, and layout to make it ready for a printer at a cost of between $100 and $300. The printer will charge $50 to $80 per 1,000 copies depending on the quantity printed, type of paper, size, etc. A lower cost method is to design your own mailer and have it printed at a quick copy shop such as Copy Cat, Postal Instant Press, Minuteman Press and others. Such printing will cost $30 to $40 per thousand. You design your own mailer by having it typed on a proportional spacing typewriter or similar equipment available in many offices. Some large headline type will be needed which you can produce yourself using Press Type or a similar $3.00 product from an art or business supply store. If you are careful in preparation, an inexpensive mailer can be as successful as a high priced job.

Addresses can be taken from club membership rosters, the telephone book, client records and other sources. You or some other person then type "peel off" labels which can be purchased at an office supply shop. I prefer to buy printed labels from a mailing list firm because they are inexpensive and because such firms have thousands of targeted lists. The mailing list firm labels will cost $35 to $45 per thousand, and you can select school counselors, boat owners, pet shops, or whatever meets your needs. Some associations have preprinted membership labels for sale, and many magazines and journals sell labels with names of subscribers. Lists of local residents should be obtained from a direct mail advertising firm in your own city or state.

As of November, 1981, first class postage is $200 per thousand if you keep the weight below one ounce — the common 20 cent stamp. You might prefer first class mail because it is simpler to use than bulk mail and makes a better impression on prospective registrants. In order to obtain bulk mail rates you must mail 200 or more identical pieces at a time, sort the mail according to zip code, and pay an initial $80 fee. The bulk mail rate (Third class, Circulars) is $109 per thousand (10.9 cents each). You will not save money with bulk mail until the reduced rate compensates for the $80 fee. Thus, I would not use bulk mail unless I were sending several thousand mailers. You only save $91 per thousand after the first thousand, and the sorting, weighing, banding and other procedures are a real bother. If bulk mail seems appropriate for your plans, visit the post office and ask for the bulk mail expert — a branch post office will not normally have such an expert. Most postal employees do not understand the intricacies of bulk mail procedures, and I advise you not to discuss bulk mail with a general window clerk or letter carrier.

Processing a mailing includes affixing the labels and postage, inserting and sealing envelopes (if you do not use a self-mailer), and in the case of bulk mail, sorting, counting, and weighing. You can process a small mailing yourself at your office or on your dining room table, but a mailing of several thousand pieces might be done by a mailing firm. The mailing firm, including some "letter shop" printers, has the automation and experience to process mailings of tens or even hundreds of thousands quickly and inexpensively. Automated equipment uses "cheshire" labels (the cheapest kind), while labels for your own manual use are known as "pressure sensitive" or "peel-off."

Of course, books can be written on these four elements of direct mail procedures, but I believe this brief description will give you the essentials. I did not mention bulk mail rates for non-profit organizations because such organizations usually are well informed on the subject. I mentioned the preparation of "copy" only in passing because it is covered in other suggestions.

45. Properly identify your prospective audience.

The key to profitability of a conference is to minimize advertising costs, and this is done by achieving the best possible response rate. Response rates are best when you properly identify your prospective registrants. Money and time are required to inform your potential customers. By targeting your information to the potential customers with the greatest likelihood of enrolling, you can reduce the volume and, therefore, the cost of the information.

Your own customers or clients can be one of your best sources of prospects. If you are an investment broker planning a conference on investments, you and your firm probably have dozens of names of clients who could benefit from more information, and perhaps hundreds of names of persons who have requested your research reports or other offerings. Another source of good prospects can be persons who have purchased goods and services related to your meeting topic. Mailing list agencies will sell you labels bearing the names of persons who have purchased investment books by mail order or who subscribe to investment magazines. Names can be sorted for a desired region or state, and if there are too many names on a list you can request a fraction of the names chosen systematically (known as an Nth sort). You might also try to obtain names directly from publishers or other business firms. For example, if you are an investment expert not working for a broker you could ask a broker for names in exchange for a fee or an endorsement.

Another method of identifying good prospects is to place posters or take-home flyers at business establishments related to your topic. Conference flyers on a farm management meeting could be placed at feed stores, farm implement dealerships and county fairs.

Association or club membership rosters can contain hundreds of names of persons interested in your topic. Special interest journals or magazines whose subscribers are interested in your topic are good advertising targets.

46. Provide complete information.

Completeness of information varies with the type of advertising and the type of reader response desired. The most complete advertisement, the direct mail piece, contains the following categories of information:

1. Title of the meeting, date, days, location, and hours.
2. Attention line such as "Repeated by popular demand."
3. The type of presentation, such as lecture or discussion.
4. Anticipated results, such as "Learn how to construct your own. . . ."
5. The speakers and their credentials — jobs, education, awards, etc.
6. Outline of the meeting including important topics and subtopics.
7. Enrollment fee, what it includes, payment policy, and refund policy.
8. The registration form with space for name, address, etc.
9. Location details such as driving directions and lodging arrangements.
10. Sponsor's name, address, telephone number and invitation to contact.
11. Who should attend — professionals or general public, for example.

The "who should attend" information is listed last because it is optional. Each sponsor must decide whether such information would be helpful in obtaining a homogeneous audience, or harmful in discouraging registrations. When you describe who should attend you are also implying who should not attend.

Periodical advertising (journals, magazines, and newspapers) is usually less complete due to limitations of space. Information might also be limited for the purpose of obtaining inquiries rather than enrollments. Some meeting sponsors prefer a large number of inquiries from persons they can later actively "sell."

47. Take care not to over-promise results.

The title of your meeting and the segments of its content should not be stated in such a way as to imply guaranteed results. This is because you cannot be certain that members of your audience will use your ideas properly. For example, it is better to use "How to Fight Inflation" than "How to Beat Inflation." In the first title you are promising that you can help the audience in their efforts; in the second you are promising them they will succeed, which is really beyond your control.

To use another example, it is better to use a title such as "How I Turned $1,000 into One Million in the Stock Market," rather than "How to Turn $1,000 into One Million in the Stock Market." The difference is in stating what you did rather than what anyone else can do. And, you had better be able to prove your claims of success.

Qualifiers such as "better" or "improved" are very helpful. These terms will make it clear that you do not guarantee total success for participants as a result of attending your meeting. Again, the complete success of participants is beyond your control, and mere improvement may be of great value.

Honesty is vital. Fraudulent claims, especially mail fraud, can mean big trouble. It is better to be a little too conservative in your promotional claims than a bit too boastful.

48. Clearly indicate what is covered by your admission fee.

Your admission fee should cover attendance at all conference sessions, take-home materials, and refreshments. Indicate in your literature which meals are included in the fee and any other benefits such as a night-before reception. Breakfasts are almost never included and are usually not mentioned. In the case of a meeting lasting more than one day, you should mention dinner arrangements even if they are "on your own."

You probably need not mention transportation costs, but to be safe you could say that participants are responsible for their own transportation and lodgings. It is helpful to include a motel or hotel rate and reservation card with your mailings or to list such details.

Transportation and lodging costs will greatly influence the appeal of your meeting, and should be considered in your site selection.

49. Provide a clearly stated refund policy.

There are three kinds of refund situations which you should cover in your meeting flyer: (1) the registrant changes plans, (2) you reject registrations due to audience size, (3) you cancel the meeting due to unforeseen circumstances.

In the first situation a paid registrant wants to back out. You should state how and when you must be notified and the percentage of the fee which will be refunded at various notification dates preceding the meeting. The purpose is to obtain earnest commitments — not to keep the money. Your advertising might state, "Notification of registration cancellation must be received two weeks prior to the meeting for a full refund, one week prior to the meeting for a 50 percent refund. . . ." I myself would not keep any part of the payment of a person who does not attend.

In the second situation you are claiming the right to limit enrollment or to cancel the meeting due to low enrollment. In these cases you routinely refund all payments. "The sponsor reserves the right to cancel registrations and make full refunds due to audience size." I feel that such a statement is preferable to mentioning "over-enrollment" and "under-enrollment." Both these terms are discouraging, especially the latter.

The third situation is rarely mentioned in conference information. It is probably best not to state a policy for nuclear warfare or earthquakes. An addition to the audience size statement might read ". . . or other unforeseen circumstances."

If you are using a registration deposit policy, you will need a separate statement on deposit refunds — a good reason to avoid deposit schemes.

50. Make it as easy as possible to register for your meeting.

A tear-off registration form or separate registration card is very convenient and is an advantage of mailed advertising. Newspaper or other periodical advertising often does not contain registration forms due to the cost of advertising space.

The registration form is a vehicle for action. It says — "Okay reader, do something." The prospective enrollee might simply hand the form to a secretary who then types a six-page requisition — but the prospect acted on the card.

You will want to encourage payment in advance, but do not insist on it. If a participant's corporation or government agency is paying for the meeting there will be delays. You want a registration card now, or a letter, a purchase order, or telephone call; worry about payment later. If you insist on advance payment, and the prospective enrollee knows it is not possible, you create a problem which can result in a rejection of your meeting. I do not recommend deposits, because those persons who cannot pay in advance usually cannot pay a deposit.

What do you do with a participant whose firm has not yet mailed their check on the day of the meeting, or the neighbor who wants you to wait until pay day? These situations anger me, but I let these participants in with a smile and treat them as if they had paid. I do not want hurt feelings in my audience. You can expect some bad debts. Even big corporations and government agencies might fail to pay you. You may later learn that "The incumbrance was not authorized."

I have never used credit cards for accepting payment, but it is done. Master Card and VISA are the services I would think of first. Local banks in your area which are affiliated with them can inform you on their use.

51. Evaluate your various forms of promotion.

In order to maximize your profits you must be able to obtain the highest tuition dollar return for each dollar of promotional costs. This is known as cost effectiveness; it is a ratio, or a comparison of dollars spent with dollars earned for each type of publicity. A simple set of records will help you determine the cost effectiveness of your various kinds of promotion — phone calls, posters, periodical advertising, and mailers.

Sources of registrations are not always obvious. A registration card from your mailings will not always be returned, especially by large firms or agencies where the accounting department uses their own requisition or purchase order forms. A registration form could come from your bulk mailings or from a person who picked up a mailer you placed in the library. The partner of a business person you telephone may not be responding to the call, but rather to a poster you placed at a retail store. Thus, you will receive some mystery checks that are impossible to trace to a certain source of information unless you telephone or write to determine the source.

You can solve many response source puzzles by keeping records of telephone calls made, personal contacts, and mailing list addresses. A better method of identification is to code your publicity, using varied colors for printed materials posted, bulk mailed, or sent to inquirers responding to telephone calls, periodical advertising, and press releases. You may wish to mark information sent to persons who inquire based on subgroups of advertising, such as three different journals.

Perhaps the simplest and most effective coding is obtained by varying your address or the name of your conference. In various promotional campaign segments you might announce a "Dog Obedience Workshop," a "Workshop on Dog Obedience," or a "Dog Obedience Training Workshop." In varying addresses, do not use the typical, obvious codes such as "Department DT" or "Department DO" for advertisements in journals named *Dog Times* or *Dog Owner*. Such coding designations insult the intelligence of prospective registrants. Instead, have some responses sent to your home, others to your office, or use subtle address variations such as J.T. Smith, John T. Smith, and John Smith.

You cannot wait until the meeting begins to ask members of the audience how they learned about your meeting because it is then too late to make adjustments in your advertising campaign, although it would help with publicity for future meetings. Also, such questions at a meeting are of no value to the audience, and therefore are a waste of their time.

You cannot rely on hunches or general impressions regarding response rates. The first two or three responses can make a greater impression on you than the 11th and 12th. You could be misled by three responses from the same source on one day which are really isolated and show no trend. You must keep records.

When you become quite expert at response source analysis you will become interested in additional details. For example, are company presidents sending employees to your meetings or are company training officers sending them? Do you get better responses from a firm if both the training officer and the comptroller, who pays the bills, receive mailers?

Again, advertising will usually be your largest expense and the most elastic. It is the most readily alterable expense. Wise spending on advertising can only result from careful, accurate response rate analysis.

52. Keep all conference notices you receive.

Over weeks and months most of us will receive numerous mailings of conference promotions and our newspapers and job-related publications will contain meeting notices. A new or expanding conference sponsor should keep files or boxes of all such information. You may wish to routinely write for additional details on all meeting advertisements.

You can obtain many useful ideas from promotional material, including design, what to include, and how to express your plans. Much of the material will have content which you find unpleasant or confusing — giving you many ideas on what to avoid.

The collection of meeting descriptions may provide ideas for topics, indicate standard practices in fee amounts, or reveal troublesome competition. You can try a different approach than that used by a competitor, offer a different format, or at least schedule your meetings in different locations.

Of course, you cannot copy the design or content of other advertisers.

SECTION SEVEN

WISE SELECTION OF
MEETING FACILITIES

SECTION SEVEN

53. Avoid public schools and some public buildings.

The selection of a meeting room is quite important. If you are to achieve high profits from your meeting by creating value and commanding high fees, you must have a prestigious meeting place with excellent furnishings and services. Many public schools have old facilities and the smell of several generations of egg salad sandwiches. New public schools have low-bid equipment and construction which is not even as good as some of the older schools.

In the minds of an audience, a public school is a place where services are "free" or of low cost, even if the meeting room is ideal. By contrast, a hotel or a motel is a place where the public expects to pay. In a public school, parents among your audience may become more interested in activities at the school than activities at your meeting. If classes are in session, there will be much noise, and meals for your participants in the cafeteria could be a real disaster.

Three types of public buildings which could be good meeting sites are libraries, city halls, and colleges. Meeting rooms are frequently of good quality in such buildings. They are prestige locations, and rentals may be low. Among the disadvantages are inadequate parking, lack of food service, and the problem of collecting high fees from an audience in a building subsidized by taxes or tax exemptions. Administrators at such sites will often display annoyance with profitability, and you might expect to be rejected for making money.

While there is a valuable benefit in having your meeting promoted as being held in City Council Chambers or Dartmore University, I tend to favor hotels and motels. I like my meeting to be wanted, not tolerated.

61

54. Insist on tables and comfortable chairs.

Meeting room furniture is very important. As conference leader you will be free to stand and walk about, but your audience will be spending lots of time seated and trying to take notes.

If yours is an informational meeting, you must have table top surfaces for taking notes and holding reference material. Tables also hold coffee cups, water glasses, ashtrays, and elbows. Tables are extremely important except in the case of some experiential groups in which participants may be holding hands, or sitting on floors. Try to arrange for tablecloths or some other sort of covering.

There seem to be three causes for uncomfortable chairs in meeting rooms. First, they are normally selected on the basis of low cost. Second, they must be very durable. Third, they must be stackable or foldable for convenience in storage and moving. The result of these three considerations is that most meeting room chairs are small, made of hard materials, usually have no arms, and have fatiguing seat and back angles.

Keep looking until you find the best furniture available, and be sure the furniture you see is the furniture you will get.

55. Avoid meeting room rentals at hotels and motels.

Some motels and hotels charge a fee for the use of their meeting rooms, and some do not. Obviously, a meeting room fee of $25 or $75 will reduce your profits if another motel charges no fee and offers meals and other services at competitive prices.

Another reason to avoid meeting room fees is one of attitude on the part of motel management. I have found that the no-charge motels and hotels need my conference to keep their food service busy and to obtain overnight room reservations. Conversely, the hotels and motels with meeting room fees seem to have all the restaurant and lodging customers they can accommodate. Thus, they do not need my meeting and may be less helpful than the no-fee establishments.

You may not be able to avoid meeting room fees if your topic requires special facilities such as access to a golf course or swimming pool.

56. Check meeting room partitions.

Motels and hotels often have movable partitions separating meeting rooms so that groups of various sizes can be served. The amount of disturbing sound that will enter your meeting space from adjoining meeting areas will depend on the amount of sound insulation in the partitions, acoustics in each meeting space, and the number of sides of your room which are temporary partitions.

You can expect a distracted audience if there are two or more poorly insulated partitions surrounding your room. Tile floors and plaster ceilings compound the problem, causing speeches and movie soundtracks from other rooms to invade your area. Real walls, draperies, acoustical tiles, and carpeting help control noise.

You must visit, inspect, and listen before making your choice of a meeting room.

57. Use a buffet line or standard menu for luncheons.

If your meeting goes through the luncheon hour you will want to provide a meal so that you can keep participants at the site and reconvene the meeting on a timely basis. I believe that the meal should be included in the admission fee, and that participants should select from a buffet table or all be served the same meal. If participants are allowed to select from an open menu, there will be varying prices and delays in service.

At dinner a buffet line will not be appropriate unless it is truly elegant. A standard dinner menu might have two or three choices rather than the one choice at lunch. Again, there should be no open menus at dinner. Section Eight contains additional ideas on dinners and evening programs.

58. Check the other scheduled use of your meeting room.

Plan to use your room for a rehearsal, for setting up equipment and material before the meeting begins, and for participants who linger after the meeting. It is very troubling to find that your 10:00 a.m. room is being used for an 8:00 to 10:00 breakfast meeting. In such a situation, your audience will pack the halls among your stacks of projectors, flip charts, handouts, and refreshments. You could then waste up to an hour setting up for your meeting once the breakfast is completed, and you will be off to a bad start.

You will need to maintain control of your room during breaks and meals, and you do not want another mob waiting outside to get into your room at the moment of your scheduled adjournment.

SECTION EIGHT

SKILLFUL MEETING PRODUCTION

SECTION EIGHT

59. Investigate accident liability

Discuss liability insurance with the manager of the motel and with your insurance agent. A one-day policy can be purchased from the agent if the motel does not offer full coverage. Other kinds of meeting sites such as churches, libraries, and public schools may not have insurance policies which cover your liability exposure and you may find it difficult to obtain full information on the insurance in force.

Will the meeting room owner's insurance protect you if a person trips over your projector extension cord, or your pot of boiling coffee falls on a member of the audience? What are the terms of the insurance?

60. Pack meeting materials in advance and in sufficient quantity.

There is no excuse for failing to bring all of your teaching aids to the meeting or bringing insufficient quantities. It seems I have been to dozens of meetings at which the speaker begins to hand out materials with the explanation, "I hope I have enough to go around." This is incompetent and inexcusable! Similarly, "We had a film to show, but there is no take-up reel so. . . ." Often there is no extra projector bulb or no extension cord.

You should have a list of all the items you will need and the items should be packed in boxes prior to the meeting. Each box should be labeled according to its contents and the session or time during the meeting when the contents will be used. Consider printing various handouts or sets of handouts on different colors of paper so that you and your audience will not become confused. It is very helpful to be able to refer to a handout by color, especially toward the end of the meeting. Participants with stacks of white paper before them will have difficulty locating the ten o'clock handout at three o'clock. (Some persons cannot distinguish green from blue.) Number identifications might also work, but not as well as colors.

Do not put handouts, name tags, and receipts in your briefcase with your lecture notes. Your briefcase will become a jumbled mess and you will not be able to concentrate on your presentation or keep the conference flowing smoothly.

Your meeting associate or clerical assistants should double check your listing and packing of materials, especially if they will be managing such items during the meeting.

Participants who pay to attend your meeting have far less patience with missing teaching aids or confusion in their use than other audiences you may have served on your regular job or in service clubs or church groups. If participants are paying you enough to earn your meeting substantial profits, you must be very thorough and professional. Unlike co-workers or club members, you will not likely see meeting participants again in a few days or weeks to make up deficiencies or to show the slides you forgot at the meeting.

61. Anticipate conflicting demands on your availability.

Last minute emergencies can interrupt carefully made plans. Are you a physician, police officer, business owner, or member of the National Guard? Assume that any emergency possible will happen, and take measures to see that emergencies will not interfere with your meeting plans.

Once your business is burglarized, your patient has a complication from surgery, your Guard unit is activated, or your police chief cancels all leaves, there is little hope of explaining that you must attend a meeting. You must make prior arrangements for other persons to be responsible for your business or professional practice before, during, and after your meeting days. Obtain prior approval of your unavailability from employers, your military reserve unit, or rescue squad. The emergency room staff or the National Guard office simply will not understand the priority of your presence at "a meeting," if not given advance notice.

62. Conduct a presentation rehearsal.

In other suggestions I describe the rehearsal of your lesson plan and the meeting team. In this suggestion I am interested in the smooth mechanical flow of meetings.

The rehearsal of a one-day meeting need not last eight hours. Each segment can be reviewed quickly in its proper sequence and be described along with related activities. "After lunch I will start the section on property taxes. Oh, John, you were to watch the meeting room during the tax part. Irene, when I talk on taxes be sure to hand out item D, it is pink, and check my accuracy when I present the calculations. Tim, don't start the tax slides until after the audience has finished their questions."

How much time does it take to hand out printed material or to move the projection screen? Can you stop the movie projector for a question, turn on the lights, write on the chalk board, then turn down the lights, and show a related slide? Each rehearsal reveals its own unique problems.

When members of an audience pay $25 to $150 per day for a conference or workshop, they expect a totally professional performance — the less they pay, the more they sometimes expect.

63. Be at the meeting site well in advance, preferably the night before the meeting.

I once began a drive from Charlottesville, Virginia to Washington, D.C. on the morning of a meeting in order to save a night's hotel room cost. A radiator hose on my automobile began to leak along a lonely stretch of rural road one-third of the way to the meeting. I had been invited to make a presentation and my absence was quite an embarrassment to me and to the meeting organizers. They were able to improvise, but if I had been the main speaker or a sponsor of the meeting, I would have stolen a car or a farm truck in order to prevent the disaster of my absence! What if a bridge is closed or there is an accident on the highway?

The important members of your faculty and staff must also arrive early. If there are local problems at the meeting site, such as an electrical failure or fire at the meeting room, you might be able to salvage your meeting if you and your staff have time to make adjustments prior to the scheduled starting time.

Just as important, most meeting sponsors will become nervous and distracted if they combine travel with planning a meeting kickoff. Even a two-hour grace period would not be enough to reassure me. You must have a rehearsal, check on your team members, test equipment, and arrange furniture. You simply cannot plan to drive up to the motel just as your clerical assistant (who may not arrive) hands out the last name tag.

64. Check all equipment before the meeting.

Each piece of equipment must be operated or inspected long before the meeting begins. If you wait until just before the meeting begins, you will not have time to make corrections or obtain replacements.

A frequently omitted item is the take-up reel for a movie projector. In most projector cases there is no space for a take-up reel and there is almost never an extra reel in the film case. Thus, the film cannot be shown unless it is allowed to run out onto the floor. Most projector cases have a holder for a spare bulb, but it may have been used or taken out for another projector. Operate the projector in the room where it will be used in order to pre-set projection angle to the screen, set focus, and find the electrical outlet. Play the film through to the end to see that it has no breaks and does not tend to "chatter." This procedure will insure that you have an extension cord, that it is of proper length, and that fittings are compatible. Use the same procedure for slide projectors, opaque projectors, and others. Check all bulbs and spares. Are all slides in the proper position in the operating tray — is there a tray?

Most motels and hotels will have a projection screen, but you cannot always depend on its condition. I once found a torn screen which had been repaired with masking tape, resulting in a dark line across the image on the screen. Check chalk boards, chalk, newsprint stands (flip charts), coffee percolators, tape recorders, and all other devices. You will often find a need for poster board, marking pens, tape, and tacks for last minute signs. Can lights be dimmed? Can a person in the back of the room read your writing on the chalk board or flip chart, or read print projected in the movies or slides? Do not forget writing pads and pens for those who fail to bring them.

If you are providing your own refreshments be sure to have a large reliable water heater and percolator, a spare, coffee, tea, sugar, cream or substitute, cups, spoons, napkins, and a small jar of decaffeinated instant coffee. Believe me, someone will ask for a cola in the morning. How long does it take for the coffee or water to get hot? Where can you get water? Will the circuit breaker or fuse blow? Who is going to bring the doughnuts? Will you need colas and cookies for the afternoon break?

If you are not familiar with movie rentals, I recommend that you visit a nearby college or university library. The library will have catalogs on thousands of free and rental films. A typical rental will be $20 to $40 for a 30-minute reel, plus you pay postage and insurance for the film's return. Free films contain advertising for a product such as a certain tea or camera. Free movies will usually be more worn. In the catalog check the designations for color, sound, date of publication, and audience age. You do not want to accidentally order a children's film. Order your film well in advance, preview it, and do not keep it too long — that is, more than three days. Try to have the college order it for you. Visit the community services office if you need additional help. They can help you borrow equipment such as projectors and tape recorders. This is a very common service of public institutions supported by your taxes.

65. Inspect the meeting site for adequate direction signs.

Now your meeting is just about to begin. Your clerks are at the registration tables and the coffee is ready to serve.

The banquet sales department will have listed your meeting on the activities board, but it might merely read, "Family Planning — Liberty Room." Since only the motel staff will be familiar with the Liberty Room, you may need to place signs of your own, especially near the registration table and meeting room door. Why have forty persons ask in turn, "Is this the Family Planning table?" "Oh, am I in the right line for birth control?"

It is quite disruptive to find that two members of your audience should be next door at the roller bearing engineers meeting after you are about twenty minutes into your presentation. The room sign is best placed on the wall next to the door or on the doorjamb if the door is left open. You will need to provide all signs for a meeting at a public building, including designation of the correct building entrance and any reserved parking.

66. Schedule a confirmation of each hotel or motel service.

If there is to be a coffee break at 10:30 a.m. your staff should make certain that it is in preparation at about 10:15. If the refreshments are running late you should hold your audience to make up the time which will be lost due to their late return, rather than try to rush the break. Similarly, before the scheduled lunch make certain that your tables are ready, and that your group can be served promptly.

You should not make meeting room arrangements in February, and then just walk in on the meeting day in April. Call or visit the motel ten days before the meeting and discuss all arrangements such as your room accommodations, equipment the motel will supply, your schedule of refreshments and meals, signs to be posted, and others. Then confirm again one or two days before the meeting. I have often found that I forgot some arrangement, or that my instructions were not made clear on the first or second visit. Someone at the motel may suggest that you worry too much. I would tell them that I make thorough preparations so that I will have no cause for worry.

Your concern for proper arrangements will protect you. For example, if one of the meetings at the motel becomes over-enrolled, one of the other four meetings may need to be moved to a small, second-class room. What you want is for the motel assistant manager to say to the manager, "No, don't move the Johnson meeting; he's been in here three times to look at this room; he'll have a stroke — move Roberts."

One of the things you can check when you visit is how to control ventilation and temperature in the meeting room — always a problem.

67. State a policy on your rights to the meeting content.

Early in the meeting and in your outline and handouts state a claim to your exclusive rights to the meeting presentation and materials. Also state a policy on tape recordings by participants, which would be "no recordings" for any meeting of mine. If your conference is one at which participants will make a sizeable contribution of information, more a meeting of peers, you should be less possessive.

Most profitable meetings provide knowledge from an expert to a group of novices. In such cases I would announce rights to the meeting content, forbid taping, and print "Copyright © W.G. Williams, 1982" on all handouts. This policy can be made clear before the meeting in your reservation confirmation form. You can easily register your entire set of printed materials and your own tape recordings by following instructions available from the

Library of Congress, Copyright Office, Washington, D.C., 20559.

68. Make announcements on checkout times, restroom locations, etc.

If your participants are to concentate on your presentation, their minds should be clear of needless little concerns such as when to check out of their rooms, where to store luggage, when lunch will be served, and where the restrooms are located. Your own concentration will be improved if you and your staff are freed from answering numerous such questions. Thirty persons with two routine questions each results in sixty needless answers.

Do you have a smoking policy? Can participants leave briefcases in the room during breaks? Will there be an opportunity for questions? Tell them before they ask.

69. Insist on punctuality at all sessions.

Your meeting will be disrupted if participants walk in late or leave early at any session. Your concern is not for the missing persons but for those who will be distracted, including you, the sponsor. Also, your meeting can deteriorate into a sort of party when members of the audience walk in and out aimlessly. If there are 35 persons at the 10:00 a.m. session, but only 20 at the 11:00 a.m. session, you have lost the attention of not 15 participants, but all 35!

If you lose control of your audience, and the participants do not honor your attendance policies, it might be that your fee is too low or that your meeting has proven unworthy of attendance. Once the meeting begins you cannot change the price or replace the audience, but you can manipulate the content to make it more valuable. More on this in Sections Nine and Ten.

You should express your interest in full and prompt attendance beginning with your promotional literature. One meeting sponsor prints the message "We Mean Business" in all advertising.

I try to be understanding and tolerant of all aspects of audience behavior except tardiness and absenteeism. When a person misses my session, is late, or leaves early, I can be very impatient!

70. Record your meeting with a reel-to-reel tape recorder.

A recording of your meeting including all presentations, comments, questions, and answers, can be quite valuable if you later plan to sell recordings, franchise your meeting, or write a book. The recording can also serve to verify your version of the meeting content in the event that a participant at a nutrition meeting, for example, later claims that you told the audience that quinine water will cure cancer.

I stress the reel-to-reel machine because it will operate for several hours without tape changes. The changing of cassettes on small machines is distracting to you and members of the audience. You want your taping activity to be unobtrusive because many participants will be inhibited in their questions and comments if you are busily switching cassettes every half-hour.

71. Hand out materials only when they are to be used.

If you have ten, twenty, or more handout pages for your meeting, distribute them only when each page pertains to the topic you are presenting. These several distributions may seem cumbersome, but if you hand out all materials at once or in small batches of pages, your participants will be reading item 7 when you are talking on item 4. When you finally arrive at item 7, they will have lost it or will be asking questions on item 5. I have seen and heard this happen many, many times. "Stop, I don't have that one — Oh, yes here it is — No, that was number 2 — Young man, can you help me find it — No, that's okay, here it is."

The proper distribution of printed material is essential in meeting success. If you want your audience to read independently, send them to a library. Showing a movie at the wrong time would be no worse than distributing handouts at the wrong time.

72. Provide evening programs at meetings lasting two days or longer.

If participants are staying overnight for a presentation on the following day, you should provide a dinner and an evening program. There could be a prestige dinner speaker or some other light session. Evening hours are especially good for slide shows or movies related to the meeting topic.

Among the persons who attend your meeting will be many who might feel you are wasting their time if they merely return to their lodgings to watch television after dinner. Dinner "on your own" is even worse. Some participants will use their empty hours for drunkenness and pranks such as putting detergent in the motel fountain, or worse. Again, I warn beginners to avoid multi-day meetings. I can recall a very rowdy evening at a three-day conference at a Vermont resort. After dinner there was a drinking match, a canoe race across the lake, running down halls banging on doors — and most of us were in no condition to attend the next morning's sessions. It was obviously a memorable experience, but I am glad I was not the meeting sponsor.

An evening meal and program require some announcements of expectations. Ralph will want to get into jeans. Jim will change into his best suit. Anne will wear a special evening pants outfit. State some hints on attire and allow time for preparations. If there is to be a sponsored cocktail hour or cash bar, schedule it just before dinner so it will come to a close.

Evening sessions should be especially interesting and attractive to encourage the greatest possible attendance. Similarly, the early morning and late afternoon segments should be irresistible. The common practice of putting the least beneficial topics at the beginning and ending of the day of the conference only encourages absenteeism.

73. Provide a take-home packet.

Most participants will be disappointed if they do not have a packet of materials to take home. There is something symbolically sterile about leaving a meeting empty-handed. Also, participants who are not quite fully pleased with the meeting might find some solace in taking a full folder back to colleagues or to read themselves.

Unmarked conference folders can be purchased inexpensively from office supply firms, and each participant can insert the conference schedule, audience roster, handouts, and written notes.

Custom-printed folders are very impressive. Have the topic and your name or organization name printed, but not the date or location so that the folders can be used on several occasions. If no local store can provide printed folders contact such firms as Crestline, Inc., 18 W. 18th Street, New York, NY, 10011, or Day-Timers, Allentown, Pa., 18001. Printed folders are just slightly more expensive than plain drugstore-type folders. The cost should be 35 to 45 cents each.

SECTION NINE

EFFECTIVE MEETING CONTENT AND DELIVERY

SECTION NINE

74. Prepare a lesson plan, rehearse it, and do not read anything.

Your lesson plan should include all topics to be covered and enough notes to keep your ideas flowing smoothly. The notes could be key words which will refer to sentences and paragraphs in your presentation. The lesson plan is for your use, not for distribution.

When you begin each session you must know exactly what content will be included, based on the key words or key ideas in the plan. The lesson plan should not contain written content to be read, except perhaps for a few quotes. Reading at a meeting is at best boring. Ability to read aloud well is a rare skill, especially hour after hour. Perhaps the greatest problem with reading is that a reader is unable to think about the topic and be responsive to the audience.

A lesson plan with notes will insure that you cover the information you had planned to use. You can also improvise by lining out key words and adding others depending on the needs and interests of the audience.

The rehearsal will help you judge the amount of time required for your presentation, and will give you practice in expressing your ideas. As you rehearse, you will be able to correct flaws in the notes and gain practice in following them. This practice will result in a sort of programming of your memory which will be a big help in your meeting. It is important that you actually talk through your presentation — not just review the notes. You might wish to record part or all of your rehearsal. Be sure to allow time for audience questions and comments. This rehearsal is separate from the team rehearsal.

If a meeting is not purely informative, but rather offers activities and encounters, your presentation rehearsal will be simplified, but you must gain practice in the conduct of the activities. You cannot simply list "Audience role-play on parenting situation." You cannot wait to see what will happen; you must try the role-play situation with rehearsal characters, unless you have used the situation previously.

75. Arrange presentation style and audience seating to suit conference goals.

If your goal is to convey large amounts of information, you should use a lecture presentation with some variety such as different presenters, movies, or demonstrations. Your podium or speaker's table should face the tables and chairs of the audience which can be set in arched rows so that persons on the ends are not distracted. The informational meeting requires a writing surface, preferably tables. Table space also is useful for computations and reference material.

If your goal is to conduct a discussion, to share ideas among participants, or solve attitudinal problems, you will have little cause for lecturing and thus it is important that members of your audience be able to face one another. A circle of tables and chairs or a horseshoe arrangement is suggested for this type of meeting. I do not like chairs alone — it almost would be better to sit on the floor or on a lawn than to have chairs without tables.

76. Be yourself.

Your meeting preparations should not include an attempt to become an actor or actress. Even if you are able to develop an act, you will soon return to your natural personality under the stress of the meeting process. This transition from one personality to another will confuse your audience, and undermine your leadership.

If you are a humorous person, laughs will occur without planned jokes. If you are not naturally "funny" you should make no attempt at humor. Failed attempts at humor can be very humiliating. I will, however, tell you of one joke for a meeting which is almost always successful. The meeting starts and you have made some preliminary announcements. Then you say, "I hope you don't mind if I start off with a couple of dirty jokes." Pause. "I'd like you to meet my associates John Doe and Jane Doe." They both stand as their names are called, amid laughter from the audience, hopefully.

If you are not naturally a dynamic, charismatic speaker, do not try to put on a dynamic, charismatic act. Rely on sincerity, thoroughness, eloquence, conviction, or whatever is your own special quality. It is difficult to fool just one person, even briefly, with a phony act. It is impossible to fool an audience of thirty or more persons for six to eight hours.

77. In the delivery of your conference message, concentrate on density, flexibility, and elasticity.

Content density means that you have valuable information and plenty of it. One of the most common causes of meeting failure is a meager offering of content. Try to reach a point in your planning where you can say to yourself, "They will be astonished at how much they will learn — I have enough here for two meetings!"

Flexibility is the capacity to drop or add content to suit the special interests of your group. If participants at a writer's workshop are more interested in copyrights, royalties, and publishers' contracts than they are in manuscript preparation, the meeting sponsor should be able to make the needed adjustments. However, the meeting sponsor may know best what the audience needs to learn. For example, if manuscripts are not well prepared there may be no copyrights, contracts, or royalties.

Elasticity refers to your ability to change the pace of the meeting, depending on whether most of your audience is unable to keep up with your content, or the opposite, are wishing you would increase your speed of presentation. Experience will teach you how to judge your pace. As a beginner, you can ask your audience or your meeting associate. You can also observe indications in the audience such as requests to go back to explain old material. If you decide to slow down, it is best to omit minor bits of content from each session, rather than to reach the end of the meeting without covering all the sessions you advertised or included in the outline. Participants will be very unhappy if you list eight session topics and deliver only six. Conversely, you cannot quicken your pace throughout the meeting without having a reserve of material to add. Thus, you should prepare an optional session to add to your meeting. Participants will be almost as disappointed with an early adjournment as with a missing session.

How often I have heard confessions by a meeting sponsor such as, "Gee, I'm sorry we couldn't get to the last session on what to do if everything else fails." Or, "Well, it's only three o'clock, does anybody have any idea what we can do now?"

78. Furnish an outline of your meeting.

It is important that members of your audience have an understanding of the overall content of your conference, where they are in the program at any hour, and how the various segments fit together. The outline should be one page or less. This will include the title of each session and perhaps two or three sub-topics for each session. The outline should not occupy much reading time or furnish so much advance information as to make your presentation seem redundant.

Listings in the outline should be interestingly worded so that participants will have something to look forward to. If the outline is intriguing, you will have good attendance at each session. If some members of the audience become slightly bored with session three, the anticipation of session four might keep their interest alive. For example, rather than list session four as "Legal Considerations" it would be better to list it as "How the Law Can Work for You."

79. Base your meeting content on forty, sixty, or more key concepts.

Unhappy participants will often state that they are not sure what they learned at a conference. A satisfied audience, by contrast, will leave a meeting with the feeling that they have gained dozens of key concepts, together with scores of supporting ideas. The presentation of key concepts will increase the retention of content and boost the audience's appreciation of the meeting. Such an organization will also help with your lesson plan preparation, and will help insure content density.

This organizational structure must be made obvious in your presentation. For example, "Our 23rd key concept in property management is to acquire good tenants by telling your best apartment renters of any pending vacancies." You can also list the keys in your handouts for each session. This will enable your audience to separate essential information from supporting information. If participants could make such distinctions for themselves, they probably would not need your meeting.

Obviously, this book you are reading is organized in a key concept fashion. Try it; buy a pack of note cards and take several long walks and think of all the important elements you have learned about your topic. In your mind, review your training and events you can recall as having been important lessons for you. Write a key concept on each card, and then arrange the cards in a logical sequence. Later, fill in details for each concept.

80. Be certain you are prepared to present the core of your content.

This is an elusive suggestion to understand fully and examples might be the best way to present it. Have you ever read a magazine article or watched a television program which makes the following kinds of statements?

"In making a wise investment be certain that you will not lose money."

85

"Prepare your job resume so that it will get you the position you want."

"Jams and jellies should not be preserved in such a way that there will be contamination."

These statements are superficial. "If you want to go forward, be certain not to go backwards." "If you want good jelly, don't make bad jelly."

A superficial statement may be a good start, but you must be sure to add the Who, What, When, Where, Why, and How. Sure, the way to better nutrition is to eat wholesome food and to avoid unwholesome food. Name the foods. List their nutritional content. Describe the preparation which best retains nutrients. What are the sources of such foods? How does one balance the nutritional attributes of a variety of foods?

81. Be cautious in your use of examples and anecdotes.

There are two problems which can occur in the use of examples and anecdotes. First, they are often used without a proper conceptual foundation — the speaker knows the value of the story, but the audience may not. Second, they often bring unrelated information or emotions into the discussion.

At a meeting on coaching, a certain coach's career might be used as an example of success. "He started as assistant coach at Wilson High School and was later head coach at Lincoln High and Banner College where he had the best win-loss record in the country at age 32," and so on. The audience has learned nothing about coaching.

I once was attempting to make the point that training equipment at schools should be similar to job equipment, and I used an example of a drafting student who could not use the equipment on his first job. Well, there were two drafting teachers in the audience who wanted me to know that there was nothing wrong with drafting education. Some business owners said they were not going to hire students until they had work experience. My example obscured the concept I was trying to illustrate.

86

I know of a real estate lecturer who described several transactions in which members of his audience had been involved. They were very angry at having their business made public.

82. Guard against contradictions.

You can be seriously embarrassed and lose the respect of your audience if you present contradicting information or advice. For example, do not recommend municipal bonds in a morning session and then criticize them in the afternoon.

When you are attempting to show the pros and cons of an idea be certain your audience understands that you are not contradicting yourself, but rather are attempting to show that an idea has a mixture of advantages and disadvantages. A municipal bond may not earn high interest, but earnings are free of Federal income taxation, for example.

Study your outline, lesson plans, handouts and rehearsal for any signs of contradictions. If there is to be more than one speaker, their content should be consistent unless it is your announced purpose to present differing viewpoints.

83. Avoid redundancy.

Repetition of important information can be a valuable reinforcement for effective learning. By contrast, redundancy occurs when information is repeated without purpose, causing boredom and wasting time.

When you repeat ideas, demonstrations or other parts of the program you should do so with a good reason. Perhaps your concept is difficult to convey and to understand. The audience might have asked if you would "go over that again." Speakers are often redundant because they have little to offer and a long time to offer it.

You will want to repeat many of your key ideas, just as I have repeated many — such as the suggestion to not give away your meeting topic idea. You must not fail to protect your meeting idea, so I remind you.

84. Establish a formal attitude toward accuracy.

Most of us make dozens of casual statements every day. We speculate and give hunches. For example, a neighbor's lawnmower will not start and over the back fence we may suggest a new spark plug, without any real evidence for such a diagnosis. A friend announces he has $10 on the Baltimore Colts and we respond with a strong opinion that the Colts cannot possible win Sunday's game.

In a paid admission meeting which the sponsor has promoted as being of great value, there must be strict attention to accuracy. If you are expressing personal opinions, make this clear, and try to show the reasons which caused you to reach the opinions, or describe their supporting logic. If you are conveying facts, you should be able to prove their validity.

Humor and sarcasm can cause problems of accuracy because they are potentially confusing. For example, at a tax seminar you are asked if a person can deduct most restaurant meals with friends on the basis that such meals are providing skills needed later to entertain clients. You consider this to be ridiculous and say, "Sure, but the doggie bag must be subtracted." Among fifty persons in the audience, two will think you are serious; another writes down every word and is not "reading" your face. So, in effect, you have provided false information to them on their tax computations and the IRS.

85. Use a variety of speakers, presentation formats and media.

Six or eight hours of watching the same person present a single type of program makes for a very slow day. Participants need variety such as a new speaker, a slide show, a demonstration, or another change of pace. If you have several pace changers such as movies or slides, try to arrange your program so that they are not all used in the same part of the schedule.

86. Limit the use of demonstrations and exercises.

Demonstrations or audience activities can provide a refreshing break from a lecture and can greatly enhance learning. However, they should not be used as fillers to mask a lack of real content.

If you are conducting a tax preparation seminar you may wish to distribute forms for completion. In order to save time you could have the audience begin to work on the forms and then take them home for completion and comparison with model forms you provide at the end of the meeting. Full completion of the forms or any other problem set at the meeting will result in boredom of the quick workers, frustration of the slow workers, and time wasted by all.

At a solar energy conference you may wish to show all of the components of a solar collector and how they are assembled. This demonstration could require ten minutes or two hours, depending on how well it is planned. In a fast demonstration you would have a collector assembled, but not fastened (not soldered, nailed, etc.). All the pieces would come apart easily and each could be labeled. If you tried to build all or part of a collector from uncut lumber, tubing, and other parts, you would have a lengthy demonstration.

Be certain all members of your audience can see your demonstrations, especially if they are conducted on the floor. Are demonstrations and activities necessary to convey your information? Is all of the time devoted to them really productive?

87. Avoid subgroups, or buzz groups.

At many conferences and workshops the audience is divided into small groups for discussion or to tackle a single part of a topic. Commonly, the subgroups will report back to the full audience on their deliberations. Almost always such subgroups are a waste of time, both in their meeting time and in their reporting time. They are often used as a distraction to hide the lack of content in a conference program.

In most cases, when I am at a meeting I hate to hear the leader say, "Okay, now let's divide up into groups." Such a leader is often eager to end the full exposure of his ineptness. There may be only two hours of content for the seven-hour meeting. So, the sponsor lets the participants entertain each other.

In a consensus building meeting, or one designed to share information, there could be some justification for subgroups, also called buzz groups. However, the persons in groups A, B and C are missing the benefits of group D. If there are four subgroups, each participant is missing three-quarters of the experience. The subgroups usually have no plans or preparation and will not achieve the results expected in a high-priced, money-making meeting.

Before using subgroups ask yourself if they are essential to the success of your meeting. Or, are you actually using group work as a filler, because you lack content and confidence, and just want to get the audience off your back?

SECTION TEN

UNDERSTANDING THE MEETING AUDIENCE

SECTION TEN

88. Decide what you would expect from a meeting you attend.

A helpful planning strategy I have used is to make an informal list of what I appreciate and do not appreciate in a meeting at which I am a member of the audience. For me, I like to leave a meeting with pages of notes and handouts I can use for later reference. I like to have my questions answered at the meeting, and I will be very dissatisfied if I leave a meeting with an unanswered question on my mind. I want to know the other participants at the meeting along with their addresses and telephone numbers for future contacts. I do not like to have other members of the audience waste the presenter's time with inane questions and comments. I like tangible, useful ideas even if I disagree with them, rather than to hear vague, pulpy philosophies. If I pay $50 for a meeting, I want $500 worth of practical ideas I can hardly wait to try.

I like a few laughs, a decent meal, and no discomforts such as hard, armless chairs. A location convenient for transportation is a plus, and I want to be treated as a respected guest. I want to be inspired, not burdened by cynicism.

Now, make a list of your own, and begin to think of your meeting from a consumer point of view.

89. Introduce participants.

It is essential that you allow participants to introduce themselves at the beginning of a conference. Name tags are also valuable, in addition to a printed roster of participants.

During the introductions all persons should have an opportunity to state their names and professional affiliations. More important to the conference leader are the participants' prior training and experience in the meeting subject area, as well as their particular areas of interest. The introductions give the participants attention and recognition; if they are to accept you, you must first accept them.

A printed roster of participants also provides recognition, but it has two other important benefits. First, a roster with names, addresses, and telephone numbers allows persons at your meeting to develop future contacts on topics of interest. These contacts alone can be worth your admission fee. Second, if the list is typed after seating, it becomes a sort of name map which is a big help in converting your audience from a group of strangers to a group of acquaintances. In this roster building procedure you send note paper across each row for participants to list their names; then a typist adds registration data such as addresses, and makes copies of the list for distribution.

90. Base audience participation on audience status and meeting goals.

If you will be lecturing on a topic as an expert and your participants are beginners, your goals and their status are such that members of your audience will have little to say other than to ask questions. If, however, your meeting purpose is to solve a shared problem, change attitudes, or build a consensus, there could be much discussion and lengthy comments from the audience.

You will waste audience time if you are an expert treating beginners as equals. You will antagonize your audience if you are one expert lecturing to many other experts. For example, if you are a sales expert leading a conference for experienced sales agents, your audience must be able to share and contribute. They will not sit quietly, taking notes, and nodding their heads in reverent approval, as might a group of sales trainees.

91. If you ask for suggestions be certain to use them or obviously consider them.

In your introductory remarks you should ask for suggestions and questions from the audience, and this request should be repeated throughout the meeting. Also, you must give careful attention to questions and comments. All questions should be answered if they are within the scope of the meeting. If you have no answer just admit it and continue with your presentation.

Comments should be given recognition — "Thank you for sharing that idea." A comment or suggestion you cannot endorse should be treated respectfully, but should be politely dismissed so that your position is made clear. "That's an imaginative idea, but based on my experience. . . ."

Repeat all questions, suggestions, and comments offered by the audience so that you will be certain you understand them and to be certain each member of the audience has heard them.

If you curtly reject your audience, you can expect them to reject you.

92. Provide times for questions and comments.

Long questions or comments and those which tend to introduce new subjects should be limited to periodic times set aside for this purpose, usually at the end of each hourly or half-hourly session. Your meeting associate can help answer these questions while you take a break and plan for the next session. The associate could also fill in details on an explanation you did not present clearly.

At any point during your presentation you should be responsive to brief questions or comments which will assure audience understanding of your message. I once used the term "boom vang" in a sailboating lecture. "B" and "V" are sometimes difficult to distinguish in a spoken presentation, and one person asked me to spell the term. Spelling aloud did not help much, and another person asked me to write the term on the chalk board. As I wrote the letters I noticed that most of my participants were taking notes. Few had understood me! If I had placed a restriction on such little questions or comments, I really would have been talking to myself.

93. Anticipate quirks of group behavior.

In any group of twenty-five, forty, or more persons there may be a comedian, a sleeper, a showoff, a know-it-all, an instigator, a slow learner, and various other personality types. There might be a person who seems to pay absolutely no attention to the program despite having spent the time and money to attend. There may be a person who will ask seemingly endless questions or who will offer numerous comments or isolated personal experiences. There may be several conversationalists muttering in the back of the room. There may be a distractor who attempts to change the focus or the direction of the meeting.

Each of these characters can be tolerated and often enjoyed if their behavior is moderate, but if one or more becomes an obstacle to the success of your meeting you must find a solution. Those who seek attention, such as the comedian, the showoff, and the know-it-all, should be given attention. You can ask them to stand and give their views or share their joke. They might be asked to help with the meeting by distributing handouts or operating a projector. Fire a difficult question at them from time to time.

Slow learners should be given extra help during breaks, and your associate can sit near them to offer assistance. A sleeper or those holding private conversations should also receive special visits from your staff, or you can ask them questions.

When a person attempts to change the focus of your presentation it might be a signal that others in the audience have similar, but unexpressed interests. If the change of focus seems unwise, say that you believe the meeting will be more productive if you do not alter the content; then read the faces of the group to see if they agree, or ask them. The change may be minor, have value, and be the consensus of the group, in which case you make the change. You can-

not, however, let one or two participants overrule your best judg-
ment or allow them to speak for the majority.

The participants with the frequent five-minute questions or obscure personal reflections are the biggest problem for me. They
seem at times to be completely oblivious to the flow of the meeting
and to be inconsiderate of the valuable time they are wasting for
others in the audience. Often you can anticipate the crux of their
question or comment and sum it up for them quickly. "So you're
saying that these three experiences and others you may have had illustrate the importance of personal contacts in having land re-
zoned." You can also avoid their lengthy question or comment by
offering a private conversation at the next break or at lunch.

In all of your group behavior controls you must not alienate your
total audience by demonstrating intolerance or hostility to an individual, especially before the group itself has recognized a problem.
The audience may enjoy the group comedian at first, or find the
know-it-all to be helpful in the beginning. Use good timing — do
not try to solve a problem until it is perceived by the audience.

94. Be prepared for disagreements.

Disagreements with anything you say or do at the meeting are a
natural part of group behavior. There even may be persons at the
meeting who have planned to introduce counter-opinions.

The first step in managing disagreements is to give recognition
to the disagreeing participant. You respect this person; you respect
the counter-opinion; and you respect each person's right to reach
individual conclusions. You show respect by paraphrasing the ob-
jection — "Mr. Thompson believes that municipal bonds are a dangerous investment because he foresees a collapse of local governments in economic or social hard times." The second step is to get
the meeting moving again by pointing out that you have many
other ideas that you do not want the audience to miss — or have a
chance to disagree with!

The planned presentation of counter-opinions can occur at

almost any meeting, but is most likely when there is an obvious controversy with vested interests. I have registered employees of electric utilities at a solar energy meeting. They were seriously interested in becoming better informed or in learning what the audience was being told. They were, however, not easily indoctrinated. It would not be a big surprise to find a Federal or local revenue agent at a tax tricks meeting, or a school system representative at a workshop on how to obtain better educational services for handicapped children.

If you face disruptive levels of dissension from an "infiltrator," you might ask the audience to confirm your suggestion that the majority will be denied the benefits they paid for if the meeting plan is obstructed. That is, you isolate the troublemaker.

95. Periodically take stock of audience reactions.

Is the attention of your audience drifting? Are they rebelling? Do they seem frustrated or tired? Are they still asking questions on the 10:00 a.m. topic at 11:30? Are they talking among themselves or reading newspapers?

If participants are bored, you are off their subject interest or moving too slowly. If they are frustrated, tired, or asking old questions, you are presenting your content too quickly or explaining it poorly. If they are rebellious, you may be presenting numerous controversial views without convincing foundations.

In any event, you can adjust better than they can adjust. An unscheduled break can help, during which you casually ask one or two persons how they think the meeting is going. Ask your associate and staff for suggestions. Try moving furniture or showing your movie earlier than planned. A segment to be presented by another speaker could be rescheduled in order to break the spell.

If I were to risk making an error, it would be on the side of working my audience too hard. The quick presentation of two or three difficult concepts will either press them to attention, or offer evidence that you had already been trying to do too much too fast.

I do not suggest that you stop a meeting and turn to a troubled audience for advice on how you should manage the meeting. I have seen this done and it does not often succeed because you will surrender leadership and present an additional task for the group to accomplish.

96. Consider offering follow-up contacts.

You may be interested in the satisfaction or benefits of keeping in touch with members of your audience. Perhaps you are available for private consultation. Or, you may ask participants to inform you of their success in using your ideas. You may also ask them to inform you of new ideas they develop on their own after the meeting. You might offer to mail a newsletter containing new ideas.

Personal contacts are an important byproduct of your meeting and I would make an effort to develop continued contacts. At least be certain to include your name, address, and telephone number on your outline and handouts. Post-meeting contacts can enhance your future conferences, consultation, and publications.

97. Conduct a participant evaluation of your meeting.

An evaluation form should be distributed as the final presentation of your meeting. You thank the participants for their time and attention and wish them continued success in their activities. Someone should collect the forms at the door as members of the audience depart.

Evaluation responses will help you improve future meetings and will give participants an opportunity to render favorable and unfavorable judgments. This pressure release function of evaluations is important. Without an evaluation the strongest impression left in the minds of your audience may be frustrated feelings of not having been allowed to have the last word.

SECTION ELEVEN

MEETING TECHNIQUE CHECK LIST

SECTION ELEVEN

Money-Making Meeting Check List

Number	Suggestion	Notes
1.	Develop an understanding of the money-making meeting concept.	
2.	Consider the earnings potential of a money-making meeting.	
3.	Understand the investment advantages of money-making meetings.	
4.	Compare other ways to sell your knowledge.	
5.	Consider the possibilities for follow-up earnings.	
6.	Identify your type of meeting.	
7.	Assess the value of your topic.	
8.	Assess your knowledge or talent to be offered for sale.	
9.	Assess your teaching skills.	
10.	Do not explore too far for a conference topic.	

Number	Suggestion	Notes
11.	Assess your leadership skills.	
12.	Assess your credentials and your reputation.	
13.	Consider assisting another meeting sponsor.	
14.	Investigate organizations and agencies related to your topic.	
15.	Study the conference competition.	
16.	Consider some of the negative ramifications of your meeting.	
17.	Do not talk about your exact plans.	
18.	Limit your publicity.	
19.	Be prepared to take full advantage of your meeting idea.	
20.	Become a meeting expert.	
21.	Start in your own city or state, if appropriate.	
22.	Consider the disadvantages of a local site.	
23.	Select distant sites based on population centers, transportation centers, and interest centers.	

Number	Suggestion	Notes
24.	Avoid conference sites near state or other governmental boundaries, in some cases.	
25.	Choose a good response rate month.	
26.	Find out how to conduct business in distant areas.	
27.	Avoid scheduling conflicts.	
28.	Consider a time and site which serves participants at another meeting.	
29.	Choose a productive daily and hourly schedule.	
30.	Plan for optional meeting days.	
31.	Appoint a meeting associate.	
32.	Employ one clerical assistant for each thirty participants.	
33.	Appoint a local coordinator for distant meetings.	
34.	Involve other helpers in your meeting.	
35.	Avoid partners or association presentations.	

Number	Suggestion	Notes
36.	Consider the advantages and disadvantages of "experts."	
37.	Hold a rehearsal for the meeting team.	
38.	Estimate your front money.	
39.	Estimate your production costs.	
40.	Make adjustments for maximum profits.	
41.	Set your fee so as not to belittle yourself or your audience.	
42.	Start with limited promotion and escalate as needed.	
43.	Schedule your promotion to last approximately four weeks, ending four weeks prior to the meeting.	
44.	Study direct mail advertising.	
45.	Properly identify your prospective audience.	
46.	Provide complete information.	
47.	Take care not to over-promise results.	
48.	Clearly indicate what is covered by your admission fee.	

Number	Suggestion	Notes
49.	Provide a clearly stated refund policy.	
50.	Make it as easy as possible to register for your meeting.	
51.	Evaluate your various forms of promotion.	
52.	Keep all conference notices you receive.	
53.	Avoid public schools and some public buildings.	
54.	Insist on tables and comfortable chairs.	
55.	Avoid meeting room rentals at hotels and motels.	
56.	Check meeting room partitions.	
57.	Use a buffet line or standard menu for luncheons.	
58.	Check the other scheduled use of your meeting room.	
59.	Investigate accident liability.	
60.	Pack meeting materials in advance and in suffcient quantity.	

Number	Suggestion	Notes
61.	Anticipate conflicting demands on your availability.	
62.	Conduct a presentation rehearsal.	
63.	Be at the meeting site well in advance, preferably the night before the meeting.	
64.	Check all equipment before the meeting.	
65.	Inspect the meeting site for adequate direction signs.	
66.	Schedule a confirmation of each hotel or motel service.	
67.	State a policy on your rights to the meeting content.	
68.	Make announcements on checkout times, restroom locations, etc.	
69.	Insist on punctuality at all sessions.	
70.	Record your meeting with a reel-to-reel tape recorder.	
71.	Hand out materials only when they are to be used.	
72.	Provide an evening program at a meeting lasting two days or longer.	

Number	Suggestion	Notes
73.	Provide a take-home packet.	
74.	Prepare a lesson plan, rehearse it, and do not read anything.	
75.	Arrange presentation style and audience seating to suit conference goals.	
76.	Be yourself.	
77.	In the delivery of your conference message, concentrate on density, flexibility, and elasticity.	
78.	Furnish an outline of your meeting.	
79.	Base your meeting content on forty, sixty, or more key concepts.	
80.	Be certain you are prepared to present the core of your content.	
81.	Be cautious in your use of examples and anecdotes.	
82.	Guard against contradictions.	
83.	Avoid redundancy.	
84.	Establish a formal attitude toward accuracy.	

Number	Suggestion	Notes
85.	Use a variety of speakers, presentation formats, and media.	
86.	Limit the use of demonstrations and exercises.	
87.	Avoid subgroups, or buzz groups.	
88.	Decide what you would expect from a meeting you attend.	
89.	Introduce participants.	
90.	Base audience participation on audience status and meeting goals.	
91.	If you ask for suggestions be certain to use them or obviously consider them.	
92.	Provide times for questions and comments.	
93.	Anticipate quirks of group behavior.	
94.	Be prepared for disagreements.	
95.	Periodically take stock of audience reactions.	
96.	Consider offering follow-up contacts.	
97.	Conduct a participant evaluation of your meeting.	

SECTION TWELVE

MEETING RECORDS AND BOOKKEEPING

SECTION TWELVE

There are many possible approaches to record keeping for money-making meetings. Full-time meeting sponsors or those who offer meetings as a sideline to their regular business will have staff members available to design and manage record systems. Sponsors with no office staff available to them may wish to keep their own records with occasional advice from an accountant, or may hire bookkeeping services on an hourly basis to handle the entire job.

The description which follows is for informal records which would be kept by an individual meeting sponsor. It provides a foundation of meeting record knowledge which should be helpful in the design of whatever system sponsors and their accountants eventually choose.

The best way to understand records is to consider them as an "audit trail." You need to know the amount and date of all monies coming into and going out of the business, where they came from, where they went, and the product or service paid for in each transaction. You will need documentation such as invoices, canceled checks, and copies of registration forms.

Records for conference sponsors are comparatively simple because there is little or no business indebtedness, inventory, equipment, or payroll.

The first step is to open a special business checking account and use it exclusively for your conference business transactions. With proper notations it becomes an approximate business barometer. You deposit $500 or $1000 of your personal funds to start, and then your check stubs and deposit entries show the course your business finances follow.

In my case I would name the checking account W.G. Williams Seminars. If you use such names as Superior Seminars or Collegiate Conferences you will need to conduct a more extensive

113

search to be certain you are not stealing the name of another conference firm. This search and its legal implications to avoid infringement on trade name ownership can be very troublesome. Similarly, a logo you design might be similar to some trademark already in use.

The second part of the record system consists of file folders to collect and classify documentation of the transactions in the checkbook. Each time you write a check for supplies or services for your conference business you obtain a receipt or paid invoice and place it in a file folder marked Expenses 1982 (or current year). It is helpful to show the check number on each document.

Another file folder is known as Items Paid Cash. Here you will collect cash register tapes for items you cannot easily avoid purchasing with cash, such as a pen refill obtained at a drugstore. Once you have a small accumulation of cash items they can be totaled and stapled together with an adding machine tape. You then reimburse yourself with a business check, put the check number and date on the adding machine tape, and move the items to the Expenses 1982 file.

A small notebook, rather than another folder, is commonly used to record automobile mileage, taxi fares, parking fees, meals, and related travel expenses. You need careful notes with dates, times, places, and reasons for the expense. Business use of your personal automobile is recorded as odometer readings: "36108 - 36112, 4 miles, March 21, to printer." IRS instructions will inform you of the rate per mile you can deduct as a business expense, as well as the possible alternative of establishing a percentage of business use and then deducting that same percentage of all automobile expenses.

To your collection of folders we add one for office use of your home. Here are kept utility bills and rent or mortgage records. Once you establish the percentage of your home area used for office space (square footage) you then calculate the corresponding percentage of expenses for telephone, electricity, rent, etc. You also note any extra household expense caused by the business such as long distance business calls. You cannot use the office area for any other purpose. If your spare bedroom is the office, you cannot also use it as a T.V. room. If you keep clothes in the closet, deduct the square footage of the closet. I am told that home office expenses are of great interest to the IRS.

Turning from expenses to income, you should have an earnings file in which you place copies of your registration forms, perhaps alphabetized or arranged by date. You might have two sections, one paid and one unpaid. Hopefully this will become a portion of a file drawer with folders for each meeting.

Your customers will need a receipt for registration at your meeting. A registration form can be used as a receipt and also for billing purposes depending on whether it is shown paid, unpaid, or partially paid (deposit). The registration form should show the company name, the address, and telephone number. There should be a space for the name of the conference, its date, amount of payment, and balance due, if any. You might also want to provide information on your refund policy.

You can buy blank invoices to use as registration forms at any office supply firm, but they give an amateurish impression in my opinion. It probably would be better to design your own form by studying the design of the blank invoices and others you may have at your office or at home. Then use a good quality typewriter to prepare the form and take it to a printer. If you make the form one-half page in size (5½ by 8½ inches) you can have one hundred printed for several dollars at a quick copy shop. You will need an original for the customer and at least one copy for yourself.

So, now we have a special business checking account and places to keep documents showing expenses and income. It will be helpful if you can list groups of similar transactions in such a way as to provide management information and tax reporting information.

These listings can be kept in a three-ring binder (notebook) containing analysis paper. This is the light green "accounting" paper with the dark green lines. I suggest three-column analysis paper, having three columns on the right-hand side and space in the center and left for notes and dates. Index tabs for the notebook are helpful to divide the analysis paper into sections.

The first section corresponds to the income file. Here you will list each person, business firm or agency that registers for one of your meetings. The three columns, left to right, are (1) an unpaid registration, (2) a registration deposit, and (3) a fully paid registration. Therefore, the right-hand column shows a completed sale which may have been placed there initially as a paid registration or moved to the right after complete payment is received on a deposit or unpaid registration. Entries are moved to the right as the balances owed are received.

The second section of the notebook shows expenses in the categories used for IRS reporting:

Advertising	Postage
Bad debts from sales	Rent on business property
Bank charges	Taxes
Car or truck expense	Telephone
Dues and publications	Travel and entertainment
Insurance	Utilities
Interest on indebtedness	Wages
Legal and professional services	Other
Office supplies	Plus some less important
	categories

Showing each expense on its proper page enables you to know where your money is going and prepares you for completing business tax forms at the end of the year.

The third section of the notebook might be called Summaries. Here you can record the pay-back of your original investment, monthly sales summaries, refunds, and other categories you find useful.

The fourth and final section of the notebook can be used for miscellaneous information such as response rate calculations, tallies of your participant evaluations, projections of the financial effect of changes in fees, and other items.

You have probably heard of accounts payable and accounts receivable. The receivables are monies owed to you on registrations not accompanied by full payment. You can determine the status of your receivables by scanning the sales section of the notebook described earlier. You might also list your receivables in the summaries section.

Accounts payable are amounts for products or services you have purchased but for which you have not paid. I suggest that you avoid payables by taking your checkbook with you when you shop, and by pre-paying items purchased by mail. While payables have some value as short, interest-free loans, I prefer simplified records. Accounts payable can be listed in the summaries section of the notebook, and you should have an Unpaid Bills file among your files if you do not use my pay-as-you-go technique. You do not want to forget payables. They are encumbrances against your checkbook balance.

Turning now to the Internal Revenue Service, you will want to obtain copies of Schedule C, Profit or Loss from a Business or Profession, and Schedule SE, Social Security Self-Employment Tax, along with the instructions.

I also advise that you obtain these other IRS publications:

Publication 17   Your Federal Income Tax
Publication 505 Withholding and Declaration of Estimated Tax
Publication 463 Travel, Entertainment, and Gift Expenses
Publication 538 Tax Information on Accounting Periods and
                 Methods
Publication 583 Record Keeping for Small Business
Publication 587 Business Use of Your Home
Publication 334 Tax Guide for Small Business

These materials are available from your nearest IRS office. Look for Internal Revenue Service under U.S. Government in your telephone directory. Your state and local revenue offices should also be consulted. If you become frustrated with tax reporting details, a tax service or accountant can always be called upon for assistance or complete management.

You should apply for an Employer Identification Number using IRS form SS-4. This number is often referred to as a Federal Identification Number. Most state and Federal government agencies will not transact business with you unless you have the number. You should consider printing the number on your registration forms for customer reference. The purpose of the Federal registration is to prevent you from concealing earnings.

117

It is important to remember that you normally will be reporting to the IRS on a calendar year basis - January to December. I would avoid operations which span two tax years due to the record keeping complications involved. For example, do not incur advertising expenses in December for your March meeting. Try to settle all accounts for your October meeting before January. This procedure is very convenient for a conference sponsor because December is not a good conference month and January and February are scarcely better except for southern resort meetings.

I believe it is wise to keep backup records in separate locations unless you have a very good safe. Keep your checkbook, expense files, and ring binder in separate locations in order to lessen the chances that fire or theft will leave you totally without records. Keep the envelopes in which registrations arrive and print on each envelope the amount of money it contained. Store the envelopes in a separate location from your other records.

Use this separation policy for your meeting lesson plan, outline, and handouts, keeping an original and at least one copy in locations where they cannot be lost, stolen, or destroyed together. I locked one copy of the manuscript for this book in the trunk of my car, kept the working copy at home, and stored an earlier pencil version at my office. You simply cannot afford to have only one source of records and instructional material.

I suggest you buy two rubber stamps. One is to have wording such as "For Deposit Only - W.G. Williams Seminars," and is for endorsing checks. The other stamp bears your business name and address and is for use on envelopes and many other purposes.

In selecting attorneys and accountants, shop around. They do not all charge the same fee. They do not all ask for a retainer. Some will be eager for your business, others may brush you off. Some will give you lots of free information in your initial interview, others will only listen or ask you about your family. You will be amply rewarded for the extra effort it may take to find advisors who are just right for you.

APPENDICES

APPENDIX A

Packing Check List

Listed below are items commonly taken to meetings. Each meeting sponsor may have items to add. Items can be lined out if they will not be needed or if they will be supplied at the meeting site.

Pre-registration list
Registration forms
Receipt forms
Name tags
Note pads
Pens and/or pencils
Chalk board
Chalk
Flip chart stand
Flip chart paper (newsprint)
Marking pens
Sign board (heavy paper)
Tape
Tacks
Tape recorder
Recording tape
Meeting folders
Handouts (list by individual
   title)
Demonstration items (list each)

Lesson plan
Films (list)
Slides
Projector
Projection screen
Spare projector bulbs
Film take-up reel
Slide trays
Extension cords
Batteries and spares
Exhibits
Evaluation forms
Typewriter (check remaining
   ribbon)
Typing paper, correction fluid,
   etc.
Copy machine (Copy service
   in area?)
Copy machine paper
Your additional items:

For Refreshments, morning and afternoon.

Percolator, water heater, and spares
Extension cords
Ground coffee and instant
Decaffeinated instant
Cream and/or substitute
Sugar
Tea
Ice

Cups, perhaps polystyrene foam
Glasses, perhaps clear plastic
Napkins
Spoons
Plates or bowls
Doughnuts or pastries
Soft drinks
Cookies, pretzels, etc.
Your additional items:

APPENDIX B

Sample Direct Mail Advertising

The direct mail piece on the following pages is of the one-half fold design. Page 125 is the cover and page 128 is the back. One-third fold and one-fourth fold designs are illustrated. Be sure to check your initial design with Postal Service size regulation templates at any post office.

Mailer reprinted with the permission of the University of Maryland.

College Park
University College—
Center of Adult Education
University Blvd. at Adelphi Rd.

June 17-19, 1981
Wednesday, Thursday &
Friday

TRAINING THE TRAINER

How To Make The Training Process Work

THE COURSE THAT HAS TURNED HUNDREDS OF INSTRUCTORS INTO MORE EFFECTIVE TRAINERS!

"Repeated by Popular Demand"

center for management development
college of business & management
university of maryland

We'll Train You To Be A Better Trainer

We'll help you—

- Pinpoint your company's training needs . . . and zero in on them

- Set realistic training objectives . . . and meet them

- Choose the best training methodologies, tools and techniques . . . and use them effectively

- Implement your training programs . . . and

- Measure the results

JOIN US—

Learn to evaluate training methods and aids so you'll know exactly when, why, and how to use each one.

Learn how you can become a confident, skillful, resourceful trainer.

Register today.

Faculty

X. Daniel Kafcas is a Senior Training and Development Specialist at United Airlines. In addition to training managers and trainers from international and domestic airlines, he develops and conducts programs in conflict management, counseling skills and problem solving for management-level personnel. He has extensive experience in supervising employees and in field training and has served as a supervisor of Training and section coordinator for Management Identification and Development.

Dr. Michael Feldman is President of MSF and Associates of Wheaton, Illinois, a consulting firm for organizational training; and is on faculty and administrative leave from Elmhurst College, Elmhurst, Illinois. As a training consultant, Dr. Feldman has consulted with, and has developed programs for, major corporations throughout the United States as well as for public and private school districts. As the former Director of both Secondary Education and the Center For Special Programs at Elmhurst College, Dr. Feldman engaged in research in the areas of alternative learning styles and experimental learning under private foundation grants. He has held positions on both the federal and local levels of education and was awarded a United States Office of Education Fellowship in 1966, in Washington, D.C. where he subsequently served as a Program Specialist. Dr. Feldman is a member of the American Society For Training and Development.

126

Seminar Outline

I HOW TO APPROACH TRAINING SYSTEMATICALLY
- A Analyzing company training needs
- B Determining job performance requirements
- C How to match training to performance objectives
- D Writing behavioral objectives
- E Designing and developing the program
- F Gaining management commitment
- G Implementing your program

II UNDERSTANDING ADULT LEARNING STYLES
- A How do adults learn?
- B Diagnosing individual needs
- C Setting the proper environment —physical and psychological considerations

III DEVELOPING A SUCCESSFUL TRAINING STYLE
- A Personal and professional attributes
- B Strengthening interpersonal skills
  1. How do you see yourself?
  2. How do you view the trainee and vice versa

IV PRINCIPLES AND TECHNIQUES FOR EFFECTIVE LEARNING
- A Attention getters
- B Setting expectations and objectives
- C Motivating trainees
- D Building interest
- E Planning participation
- F Using repetition and application
- G Applying logic and transfer
- H Developing lesson plans

I Others

V TRAINING METHODS AND STRATEGIES
- A Demonstration
- B Role play
- C Simulation
- D Case study
- E Discussion
- F Informal presentation (indirect influence teaching)
- G Lecture
- H Group learning and group dynamics
- I Spring board motivators
- J Participatory and experiential learning
- K Goal and inquiry oriented learning
- L Questioning and response strategies
- M Individualized programs of instruction
- N Others

VI HOW TO GET THE MOST OUT OF TRAINING AIDS: When to Use Them and Why
- A Artifacts
- B Models
- C Simulators
- D Audio visuals
- E Charts and pictorials
- F Video usage
- G Film loops
- H Others

VII APPRAISING YOUR PROGRAM
- A How to construct tests to evaluate employee learning
- B Assessing test feedback
- C Modifying your training programs to reflect changing needs

210

Who Should Attend

■ Directors of training & development departments ■ Training specialists ■ Management personnel responsible for training ■ Workshop facilitators & presenters

The Manufacturing Engineering Certification Institute has approved this seminar for 6 Professional Credits (per seminar day attended) toward the SME Recertification Program.

ENROLLMENTS may be made by returning the registration form. Enrollment is limited and will be accepted on a first-come, first-served basis. Telephone reservations are also acceptable.

CONFIRMATION of your registration will be made within two weeks after receipt of your application. Information on seminar schedule, starting times and the like will be included.

HOTEL ACCOMMODATIONS are, of course, not included in the registration fee. However, if you desire overnight accommodations, please call the Center of Adult Education at 301/454-2325 for reservations.

COURSE FEE: $550, is payable to:

Business and Management Foundation of Maryland, Inc.   **TIME:** 9 AM-4:30 PM. Fee includes luncheons and all meeting materials.

CANCELLATIONS AND REFUNDS—Cancellations made less than three working days prior to the seminar are subject to a $50 cancellation fee. Refunds will not be granted after class has begun. If insufficient enrollment necessitates cancelling the course, all tuition will be refunded.

TEAM REGISTRATIONS—A 10 percent discount is automatically available for your organization if you send 3 or more people. Should you desire to send your entire team, a larger discount can be easily arranged.

TAX DEDUCTION for all expenses of continuing management education (including registration fees, travel, meals, and lodging) undertaken to maintain and improve professional skills (Treas. Reg. 1-162-5 Coughlin vs. Commissioner, 203F 2d307).

IN-COMPANY PRESENTATIONS are available. Please contact the Seminar Administrator for details.

SEMINAR ACCREDITATION—We have entered into an agreement with the Maryland State Board of Public Accountancy to meet the requirements of Chapter 02.03B. of the Regulations. For information on the accreditation of this seminar, please contact the Seminar Administrator.

For further information call: Ms. Diane Kretschmer, Seminar Administrator, at 301/454-5577.

You may receive a duplicate brochure. If so, please pass it along to an interested associate. Brochures are frequently mailed to selected lists which cannot be cross-checked against our files.

The University of Maryland actively subscribes to a policy of equal educational and employment opportunity. The University of Maryland is required by Title IX of the Educational Amendments of 1972 not to discriminate on the basis of sex in admission, treatment of students, or employment.

Please return entire panel in an envelope

Registration Form

PLEASE REGISTER THE FOLLOWING

061-210-093
TTT

Name		Title

Organization

Address

City	State	Zip

Company Phone	Home Phone

☐ Please send information about other seminars   ☐ Bill Me   ☐ Bill My Company
☐ Payment Enclosed   ☐ Purchase Order Enclosed

DETACH & MAIL TO: Center for Management Development, College of Business and Management, University of Maryland, College Park, MD 20742

Center for Management Development
College of Business and Management
University of Maryland
College Park, Maryland 20742

Non-Profit Org.
U.S. POSTAGE
PAID
University of Maryland

ATTENTION MAIL ROOM: This is dated material
Please reroute to Personnel Manager if necessary.   Not printed at taxpayers' expense. 128

OTHER FOLDS

One-third Fold   **One-fourth Fold**

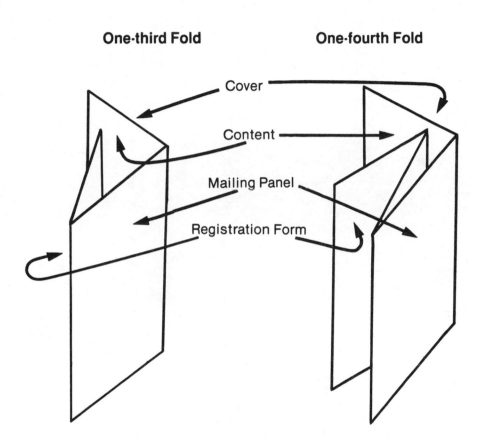

Cover

Content

Mailing Panel

Registration Form

APPENDIX C

Mailing List Firms

Following is a list of firms known to the author. *Literary Market Place* (LMP), a book available at most public libraries, contains additional sources. Most mailing list suppliers will send free catalogs, and many have toll free "800" telephone numbers.

Dependable Lists, Inc.
257 Park Avenue South
New York, NY 10010

Edith Roman Associates, Inc.
857 Avenue of the Americas
New York, NY 10001

College Marketing Group,
Inc.
Six Winchester Terrace
Winchester, MA 01890

Hugo Dunhill Mailing Lists,
Inc.
630 Third Avenue
New York, NY 10017

Education Mailing Clearing
House
600 East Marshall St.
Sweet Springs, MO 65351

Professional Mailing Lists,
Inc.
450 Seventh Avenue
New York, NY 10001

Obtain many catalogs in order to find direct mail targets suiting your own special needs. Ask local mailing firms about lists of local residents.

APPENDIX D

Sample Periodical Advertising

Four kinds of advertisements for journals, magazines and newspapers are shown on the following pages. They are presented only to show a range of possibilities, and have little creative merit. They are for demonstration only, and much of the content is fictitious.

The Tentative Inquiry Ad is used to determine the amount of interest in your meeting topic before you have the meeting fully prepared. The Free Sample Ad helps to overcome registration resistance on the part of persons who want to see what they are buying before they commit themselves.

The Scheduled Meeting Inquiry Ad is used to promote a fully prepared and scheduled meeting in situations where you wish to limit the size of your advertisement or have some other reason for wishing to communicate with prospective registrants before they enroll. It is best not to indicate the price of the meeting unless you list most of the benefits of the meeting and the full credentials of speakers.

The Registration Ad should be complete enough to obtain paid responses as well as inquiries. It will save you and the reader the extra step of correspondence or conversations. Some advertisers do not like Registration Ads because the price may discourage inquiries. These sponsors prefer to obtain leads (inquiries) from Inquiry and Free Sample Ads which they can use to actively sell the meeting to prospective registrants.

Tentative Inquiry Ad
(Teaser)

Free Sample Ad

Scheduled Meeting Inquiry Ad

A Popular One-Day Conference

SELLING YOUR KNOWLEDGE AT WORKSHOPS AND SEMINARS

Thursday March 21, 1980 9 a.m. to 5 p.m.
Hillside Inn, Montross, Ohio

CONFERENCE LEADER - William G. Williams, Ph.D., training consultant and advisor to hundreds of meeting sponsors. Williams earned his B.A. and M.A. at George Washington University and his Doctorate from Florida State University. He has held administrative posts at George Washington University, Georgetown University, and Piedmont Virginia Community College. He is the author of twelve articles and three books.

CONFERENCE TOPICS - Selecting meeting content, identifying prospective enrollees, scheduling, lesson planning, advertising, budgeting, meeting staff, printed materials, meals and refreshments, equipment, audience management, evaluation, records and bookkeeping, and much more.

REGISTRATION - The conference fee of $75, which includes luncheon and printed materials, is payable on or before March 10. Refunds honored through March 19. Meeting enrollment is limited. Lodging arrangements should be made with the Hillside Inn which is located at the intersection of U.S. routes 19 and 65 two miles south of Montross, Ohio. Telephone (123) 456-7890.

For additional conference details contact W.G. Williams and Associates, 123 Charles Avenue, Montross, Ohio 12345

Please reserve a place for me at the Workshop and Seminar Conference.

Name_____

Organization _____

Street_____

City _____ State _____ Zip _____

☐ My $75 fee is enclosed.   ☐ Payment will follow.

Please make check payable to:

W.G. Williams and Associates
123 Charles Avenue, Montross, Ohio 12345

Registration Ad

137

APPENDIX E

Meeting Evaluation Forms

Following are two evaluation forms the author has used with good results. The forms should not be more than one page in length, although you should make other changes to suit your meeting topic and audience.

The first form is perhaps the best in that it avoids the 4-3-2-1 scale and provides spaces for comments. The latter are known as "open ended" responses, which may be the best evaluations and will help the meeting sponsor in understanding the other responses on the page.

The authorship of these forms is unknown; they just crept into use and have been modified repeatedly for various purposes.

EVALUATION

(Your conference title)

PART A. Place a circle around the statement which best describes
your feelings about each aspect below.

1. MEETING CONTENT

contained all	contained most of	much material	did not provide
I needed to know	what I needed	was not covered	what I needed

2. INSTRUCTOR'S PRESENTATION OF INFORMATION

very clear   reasonably clear   rather unclear   very unclear

3. INSTRUCTOR'S ABILITY TO STIMULATE INTEREST IN THE TOPIC

stimulated interest	increased	reduced	destroyed
to a high degree	interest	interest	interest

4. INSTRUCTOR'S ATTITUDE TOWARD PARTICIPANTS

always helpful	usually helpful	often impatient	very negative
and patient	and patient	and not helpful	attitude

5. WOULD YOU RECOMMEND THIS CONFERENCE TO A FRIEND

definitely would   probably would   probably not   definitely not

PART B. Write in your ideas

WHAT CHANGES WOULD YOU MAKE TO IMPROVE THIS CONFERENCE

_____

_____

_____

_____

THANK YOU!

EVALUATION

(Your conference title)

DIRECTIONS: Please read each statement below carefully and circle the number which represents your feelings about the statement.

	Strongly Agree	Agree	Disagree	Strongly Disagree
1. The program offered me what I expected.	4	3	2	1
2. The material was presented at the proper level of difficulty.	4	3	2	1
3. I learned more than I could have on my own, reading, or other methods.	4	3	2	1
4. I was stimulated to learn more about the subject.	4	3	2	1
5. The chance to talk with other persons at the meeting was one of value.	4	3	2	1
6. The conference will help increase my competence in the subject area.	4	3	2	1
7. The meeting developed new interests for me.	4	3	2	1
8. I believe that the instructors knew their topics well.	4	3	2	1
9. The meeting topics were well organized.	4	3	2	1
10. The facilities were comfortable.	4	3	2	1

THANK YOU!

APPENDIX F

Conference Topic Suggestions

Listed below are conference topic ideas which have succeeded in the past or which have potential for future use. The topics may be too general for a single meeting and sub-specialties might best be chosen.

Time Management

Supervision

Investments
  Real Estate
  Securities
  Metals and Gems
  Other

Solar Energy
  Passive Solar
  Active Systems
  Installations
  Other

Personal Law
  Divorce and Child Custody
  Wills and Probate
  Contracts
  Criminal
  Landlord Tenant
  Other

Home Repairs
  Renovations
  Additions

How to Buy
  A Used Car
  Art
  Oriental Rugs
  Other

Nutrition

Family Health

Tax Return Preparation

Tax Strategy

Grants Attainment
  Federal
  Foundation

Persuasion

Negotiating

Sales Techniques

Business Records

Rental Property Management

Employment Search Techniques
  Resume Writing
  Interviewing
  Other

Selection and Best Use of
  Physicians
  Attorneys
  Hospitals
  Consultants
  Other

Understanding Insurance
  Health
  Life
  Liability
  Other

Home Burglary Protection

Personal Safety - Defense

Pet Grooming

Owner Maintenance and
  Repair of
    Electrical Appliances
    Yard Equipment
    Office Machines
    Other

Motivation

Marketing

Food Preservation

Organic Gardening

Genealogy

Speed Reading

Travel Planning
  General
  Specific State, Country

Office Organization

Quality Control

Time and Motion Studies

Printing and Graphics

Employee Benefit Plans
  Pensions
  Hospitalization
  Profit Sharing
  Other

Job Classification
  Compensation

Photography

Employee Training
  Evaluation

Wedding Arrangements

Drug Abuse

Parapsychology
  Precognition
  Levitation
  Telepathy
  Other

Exam Preparation
  General Test Taking
  Civil Service
  College Entrance
  Graduate School
  Other

Futurism
  Appropriate Technology
  Post-Affluence
  Discontinuity
  Other

Going Metric

Single Again

Dream Analysis

Building Codes
  Construction
  Plumbing
  Electrical
  Fire

Home Convalescence

Equal Opportunity Law

Human Relations on the Job

Transactional Analysis

Occupational Safety Law

Meditation

Starting a Business

Arbitration

Understanding Patents

Understanding Copyrights

Parliamentary Procedure

Trade Mark Rights and
  Registration

College Student Financial Aid

Operating a Consultant
  Practice

Non-Profit Associations
  Qualifying as
  Organization of
  Special Taxation

Self-Publishing or Small
  Publisher
  Public Preferences
  Editing
  Production
  Promotion
  Distribution
  Legal Aspects
  Other

Ecological Concerns
  Chemicals
  Radiation
  Land Resources
  Water Resources
  Other

Personal Financial Planning

Gaming
  Casino Gambling
  Horse Handicapping
  Bridge
  Chess
  Other

Pesticides and Herbicides
  Application
  Regulations

Unidentified Flying Objects,
  UFOs

Advertising
  Periodical
  Direct Mail
  Radio and TV
  Other

Pet Nutrition
  Health Care
  Training

Antiques
  Furniture
  Jewelry
  Automobiles
  Other

Appraisal for Homeowners

Career Planning
  Evaluation
  Change

Consumer Car Care

Furniture
  Refinishing
  Reupholstery

Home Barbering
  Hair Styling

Specialized Cooking
  Vegetarian
  French
  Oriental
  Other

Home Brewing
  Beer
  Wine

Family Planning

Crafts Workshops
  Leather
  Jewelry
  Ceramics
  Other

Energy Conservation
  Insulation

Party Planning
  Food
  Beverage
  Etiquette
  Activities

Home Chemical Safety
  Farm
  Business

Fire Safety

Chimney Cleaning

Marriage Enrichment

Horse Shoeing
  Hoof Care

Personal Development

Life Planning

Practical Data Processing
  Home
  Farm
  Small business

Natural Childbirth

Child Care and Health

Parenting

Export-Import Marketing

Mail Order Merchandising

Franchising
   Obtaining
   Sponsoring

Fund Raising

Sports Clinics
   Golf
   Tennis
   Sailing
   Other

Non-Prescription Drugs

Purchasing Administration
   General
   Printing
   Electronics
   Other

Weight Reduction

Research and Statistics
   Marketing
   Educational

Political Action Organizing

Dog Obedience

Report Writing

Homeowner Landscaping

Political Opinion
Other

Hypnosis

Management by Objectives,
MBO

Astrology

Practical Economics
   Inflation
   Monetary Policy
   Other

Vitamins

Cosmetics

Value Clarification

Stress Management

Helping Skills

Word Processing

Stopping Smoking

Library Use

Study Skills

Group Leadership

Assertiveness Training

Home Decorating

INDEX

150

Recordings 73, 75
Redundancy 87
Refreshments 41, 71, 122
Refund policy 54
Registration advertisement 137
Registration
  ease of 48, 55
  invoice 115
  receipt 115
  records 116
Rehearsal 34, 69, 81
Rental
  room 62
  movies 71
Reputation of sponsor 13
Reservations, admission 55, 116
Reserving right to content 73
Response rate
  advertising 47, 56
  time of year 23
Results, over-promising 53
Rights to meeting
  content 73
Room (See Motel room)
Rosters of audience 94
Rubber stamps 118

-S-

Sarcasm in presentation 88
Schedule conflicts 24
Seating arrangements 82
Seminar, definition 9
Signs 72

Standard menu 63
Style of presentation 82
Subgroups 89
Suggestions from audience 95
Summaries of records 116
Superficial content 85

-T-

Tables and chairs 54
Take-home material 77
Talking about plans 16
Talent to be offered 11
Targeting promotion 51
Taxes 116, 117
Teaching skills 11
"Teaser" advertisement 47, 135
Tentative inquiry
  advertisement 135
Transportation centers 22
Travel records 114
Two-day meetings 25, 76

-V-

Value of topic 10
Variety in presentation 88

-W-

Workshop, definition 9
Writer's Market 15